MULTIMEDIA : ITS APPLICATION IN LIBRARY AND INFORMATION SCIENCE

MULTIMEDIA : ITS APPLICATION IN LIBRARY AND INFORMATION SCIENCE

By
Prasanna Kumar. H.E.
and
Mahesh V. Mudhol

Ess Ess Publications

4837/24, Ansari Road, Darya Ganj,
New Delhi-110002
✆ : 3260807, 3201533
Fax : 3274173
E-mail: essess@del3.vsnl.net.in
url:http://www.essessbooks.com

First Published 2002

ISBN : 81-7000-332-6

Price : Rs. 595/-

Published by:

Ess Ess Publications

4837/24, Ansari Road, Darya Ganj,
New Delhi - 110 002
Phone : 3260807
Fax : 3274173
E-mail : essess@del3.vsnl.net.in
url:http://www.essessbooks.com

Laser Typesetting:

Mukesh Graphics

L-2/8, Mangolepuri, New Delhi
Ph. : 7924405

Printed at :

Print Line

Contents

1

Prologue

Ever since man started to record information and store it for future use, the form of information recording, storage maintenance, and channel for its usage underwent drastic challenges. The invention of paper and printing multiplied the diffusion of information. The present technological developments have made a great impact on information recording, storage, and usage. Further, telecommunication has made tremendous revolution in information handling. These changes are influencing the very structure of library and information centers. To recall the words of Veilex Robert a French Philosopher of the future " Electronic Technology is on the verge of changing society as profoundly as the invention of printing. Printing multiplied the diffusion of information in society, electronics makes possible a great diffusion in real time." He further states "It takes a couple of decades for people to get accustomed to a major invention but by the turn of the century " Telematique" will have taken hold; consumption of paper fall drastically as people communicate electronically; books will become deluxe items that people buy to show, they are cultivated, much as leather bound edition are today"[1].

Seligman Lawrence said, "I can see the technology improving to the point where in twenty years something the size of a book, perhaps could be inserted in a small video disk and read from the display"[2].

F.W. Lancaster uses the term "Paperless Society" and he far sees that the present hard copies of books will be replaced totally by the electronic media[3].

Landau described a "Library on desk" as the executive type of desk that incorporates two modules, one, a computer terminal and another a microfilm reader. The terminal is potentially connectable to any on-line retrieval system through a normal telephone system.

Thus, from the time invention of printing to the present age of electronics, variety of information storage and transmission media have found their wisdom and knowledge from generation to generation.

Libraries acquired different types of information sources for conservation and preservation of knowledge. The print media include books, pamphlets, manuscripts map, prints, plans, etc., and non-print media includes tapes, audiodisc, audio tapes, magnetic tapes, and optical technology hypermedia and multimedia based equipment. These information technologies have made greater impact on libraries and information centers. Also these have influenced and improved the library systems. It is true that the technological advances have greater impact on libraries and have changed the total scenario of libraries, drastically particularly in developed countries, but developed countries, but developing countries like India have their own limitation in harnessing the use of information technology[4].

The communication revolution is on the threshold of complete maturation as the world itself prepares for the twenty-first century with the electronics explosion, the software phenomena and the media. Communication revolution is together the most vital segment of the information superhighway that, symbolically, bridges nations and communities and thus leads to the fulfillment of the great vision of the global village.

The new communication media technologies like laser, fiber optics, telephone, teleprinter, telex television, Dictaphone silicon chip, Internet and many other telecommunication devices have come to constitute are the important component of communication media. These modern communication media have the potential to by pass several stages and sequences in the process of development encountered in the earlier decades.

Information is now flowing fast to the people through various media like print media and multimedia, The media are known to be playing an effective role not only in informing the people but also influencing their thinking and shaping their attitudes.

Communication is a fact in the world of human beings and ever counting process. Medium is the mode or form through which the message or information if communicated.

The term "Communication" has been derived from the Latin verb "Communication". Which means 'to talk together, confer, discourse and consult, one with another'.

According to John Dewey "Communication is process of sharing experience till it becomes a common possession. It modifies the disposition of both the parties who partake in it"[5].

Beltran says that, "It is both a natural and an individual demand and a requirement for social existence to use communication resources in order to engage in the sharing of experiences through symbol-mediated interaction"[6].

Simply defined, communication is the art of transmitting information, attitudes and ideas from and person to another, IT is a process of transmitting a message from a source to an audience through a channel".

Theo Haiemann "communication is the process of passing information and understanding from one person to another. It is the process of imparting ideas and making oneself understood by others"[7].

1.2. MEDIA COMMUNICATION

The message part of the communication is very important in communication media. The media of communication takes the form of symbols, words, action, pictures, numbers, etc,. The important communication media are indicated bellow:

Media are concerned with the form into which the message is placed of the various communication media, which have close relationship with library as communication agency. We will consider the following four communication media. They are:

1. Oral communication media.
2. Audio-Visual communication media.

3. Verbal or Written of Printed communication media.
4. Mass media communication[8].

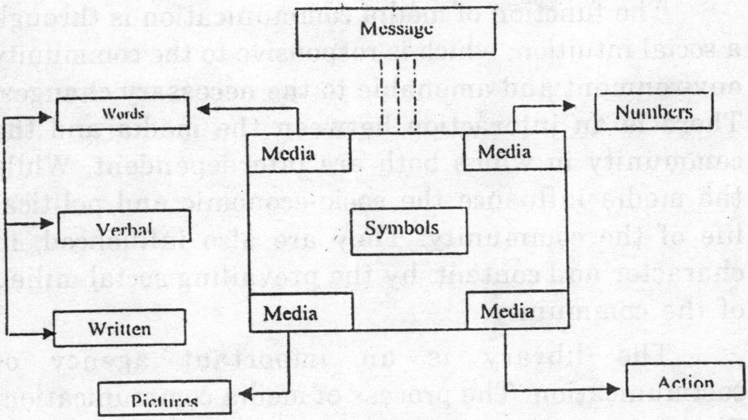

Fig. 1. Communication media

1.3. INFORMATION AND COMMUNICATION

Robert Savio distinguished 'Information' from 'communication'. According to him, information is a vertical non-interactive structure through which, a few people communicate or rather information data, information of ideas to a large number of receivers. This is a 'one-way' or 'top-down' approach, a process in which, the receivers are passive.

Communication. On the other hand, is a horizontal process characterized by interaction, this includes exchange of ideas, information, point of view, experiences, between persons and groups. In this two way process the receiver, is also a transmitter or giver. In other terms in an ideal situation of communication, passiveness is non-existent. Through, in the present context, information has the priority over communication; it is the technology that make communication both interactive astir[9].

1.4. MEDIA COMMUNICATION AND LIBRARY

The function of media communication is through a social intuition, which is responsive to the community environment and amenable to the necessary changes. There is an interaction between the media and the community in which both are interdependent. While the media influence the socio-economic and political life of the community: They are also influenced, in character and content, by the prevailing social milieu of the community.

The library is an important agency of communication. The process of media communication. The process of media communication operates in the community.

1.5. COMMUNICATION CHANNEL

Communication channel means the medium or through message passes. The words, symbols, or signs selected should be transmitted to the receiver through certain channel or medium. The media may be written media or oral media for the there are various forms written media like letters, reports manuals, circulars, notes, questionnaires etc. The farm of oral media includes face-to-face conversation, Dictaphone. Telephone, teleconferencing etc. The visual channel may be the slides, microfilms, etc television documentary films, CD-ROMs etc represent audiovisual channels[10].

1.6. MEDIA

Medium is singular and media is plural. The

term implies or means something of through which an effect is produced or is made known, mass media denote those channels of communication that reach large number of people such as television, newspaper radio etc,.

Media in relation to communication imply tools of communication. Its means the instrument or instruments adopted or applied in transmitting any message irrespective of its nature and significance.

1.6.1. Definition

Librarians have defined the term 'media' variedly. According to Harrord's Librarians Glossary and reference book media is,

"Printed and audiovisual forms of communication and any necessary equipment required to render them usable"[11].

Chambers Twentieth Century Dictionary defines media as a substance, through which any effect is transmitted or media is that through which communication is maintained. Thus media is a means that helps in the transmission of message/ information from one to another[12].

D.P.Ely in his paper "This contemporary college library change by evolution or revolution" has defined 'media' as, "Graphic, photographic, visual or verbal information or combinations of visual and verbal information".[13].

In short, media is nothing but the different types of channels namely print, sound and vision used for the transmission of messages. The transmission of verbal and visual information can be through of various means viz., graphic, electronic, mechanized and so on.

The multimedia library is one, which possesses collection of carious media several materials. These materials could include mud/clay, wood, metal leather stone, film and magnetic tape.

1.6.2. Types of Media

'Media' is a very elusive term. A medium is a vehicle of communication through which information is transmitted from a sender to a receiver. They are:

* Any of the languages, signs, sigerals, gestures or even cliches;
* Any equipment which function as a medium of communication and is used to render the media materials usable viz., radio, cassette player, record player, television, VCR, computer, CD-ROM drive, microform reader-printer, and, slide projector;
* Any physical format such as; printed records, conference proceedings, photographic records, sound recordings, video recordings, motion pictures, microforms, computer records.

1.6.3. Categories of Media

Librarian of libraries categorizes media resources into two distinct groups according to their utility. They are:

* Teaching aids used for simplifying teaching learning process, such as: maps, models, posters, charts, games, specimens, stereographs, realia, multimedia kits, globes, pictures, radio graphs and puzzles.
* Information sources and databases used for rendering reference and information services viz., reference sources, microforms, audio-visual materials, computer database, and CD-ROMs.

1.6.4. Types of Media Combinations

Media materials are prepared asking various approaches to media communications. They are:

(1) Integrated Media:

(2) Complementary Media:

(3) Supplementary Media:

(4) Independent Media:

1.6.4.1. Integrated Media

In the 'Integrated approach' Print is usually a master medium and any other non-print media such as audio, video-visual, etc., can be used as supporting media.

1.6.4.2. Complementary Media

In the 'complementary approach' decision is taken which framing the syllabus to divide the quantum of information between print and non-print media.

1.6.4.3. Supplementary Media

In the 'supplementary approach' the entire material is given usually in print but certain portions needing further information, elaboration or demonstration is given in other media formats. For example, Indira Gandhi National Open University (IGNOU) and B.R.Ambedker Open University.

1.6.4.4. Independent Media

In the 'independent approach', non-print media is used for imparting instruction to special categories of students. They can be:

Audio-Visual media for illiterate learners.

- Audio-programmes for blind learners.
- Video-programmes for deaf learners[14].

1.7. MULTIPLICATION OF MEDIA

The multiplication of media, especially the growth of public computer networks, require a complete rethinking of the scope and purpose of regulation of broadcast media. Paradoxically although the research community has been quite willing to accept new journals, and new familiar printed journals. It was highly resistant to the disappearance of the familiar printed journals. It was only in the past decade that the inevitability of this conversion process as an impact of technology[14].

1.8. MATERIALS AND EQUIPMENT SELECTION:

When involved with materials and equipment selection, the librarian needs to; be familiar with the characteristics of the various information media. The first consideration in which media form(s) is (are) best suited to a particular body of information. The ordering of the media that follows ranges from simple to complex and should not be considered is a taxonomy or hierarchy, but rather, as a means for easy identification of the form and its characteristics. The term 'mediated' refers to the equipments(hardware) necessary to give access to the information system(software).

1.8.1. Objectives

These items can be considered realia (i.e., the real thing) and includes anything in its natural state whether it is animal, vegetable, or mineral: living or preserved: original or synthesized. Skill another category is objects that representing the 'thing', such as models and replicas.

1.8.2. Visual, Still, Non Mediated Media

It includes the printed word(verbal symbols), graphics and drawings(nonverbal symbols), arete prints and illustrations and photographs(still pictures). The user of this information has direct access to it; it does not require the use equipment in order to be read or viewed.

1.8.3. Visual, Still, Mediated Media

This includes slides, filmstrips and information appearing on the CRT of a computer viewing this information requires the use of some type of electrical-optical equipment to project it onto a screen.

1.8.4. Cisual, Motion, Mediated Media

This category is the considered obsolete but warrants being mentioned. Motion picture film, in either color or block and white. The most prevalent format is the super 8-mm film packaged in either open reel of cartridge(film loop). Much less prevalent is the 16-mm silent motion picture film.

1.8.5. Audio, Non-Mediated Media

Often over looked in the library is the use of resource people who can come into the library and give talks. Musical instruments also full into this category although few libraries are involved with them.

1.8.6. Audio, Mediated Media

This includes both audio and audio tape recordings that are available in a verity of playing speeds and formats.

1.8.7. Audio, Still, Visual, Mediated Media

Sound filmstrips and sound slides fall into this category, the usual(filmstrips and sound slides are discrete entities and must be viewed on some type of optical projection equipment, whereas the audio(disc of tape) require some kind of electronic play back.

1.8.8. Visuals, Motion, Audio, Mediated, Media

This category includes the sounds the sound motion picture film in either block and white co and is predominantly available in a 16-mm format, although some producers offer the option of obtaining certain titles that are available in super 8-mm, TV is also in the category.

1.8.9. Consumable Media

Includes are items are in constructed or compounded by the patron and cannot be return to their original state, coloring, books, and textbooks or work books in which it is intended the user will write.

1.8.10. Manipulative Media

Games, simulations, teaching machines, and computer terminal, fit into this category. these are essentially devices that patrons, either singly or in small groups, have to manipulate interact with in order to obtain information[16].

1.9. MAJOR CATEGORIES OF MEDIA

Libraries are involved in a wide range of media, and the librarian needs to be aware of the various media categories. The task of learning the various media categories is quite simple, and indeed most people are familiar with most of them as an integral part of their every day lives. The benefit of such learning is realized when librarian becomes involved in selection and needs to know what medium is best for a particular need or situation. The following categories, they are:

1.9.1. Art Prints

An art prints is either an original work of art(a painting) or a facsimile. The value of art prints is basically twofold: They can be used for studying the styles and techniques of various artists, or they can be loaned out simply for their homes quite often become regular users of these service. Some libraries integrate art prints into the picture file collection.

1.9.2. Books

Most books in libraries are bound with hard covers; however, paperback books are becoming more prevalent: Reference books and more specifically encyclopedias, are generally available in hard cover. Selection aids are also available in book form, both hard cover and paperback. Books are also classified as fiction or nonfiction. A more specific classification is that of a textbook.

1.9.3. Community Resources

Community resources include things available in or from the community and fall into two major areas (a) Thing in the community that cannot be brought in to the library, but must be seen on actual location and would be classified as field trip items; and (b) Things from the community that can be brought into the library and would be called local realia.

1.9.4. Computer Software

Computers, more preciously microcomputers are becoming more prevalent in libraries CD-ROM is becoming a library mainstay. Currently there are thousands of programs available for all brands of microcomputers.

1.9.5. Filmstrips

A filmstrip is a continuous strip of photographic film containing a series of still pictures intended to be viewed separately.

1.9.6. Kits

A universally accepted definition of the term kit is lacking because procedures of kits do not use the term the same way. It will have to suffice to say a kit is a collection of package of two or more items on a particular topic. Therefore if a procedural packages two of more items and calls it a kit. Perhaps a true kit would be a multimedia kit.

1.9.7. Maps and Charts

A maps or chart, for the purpose of definition as a single, unbound discrete item capable of being examined as a complete entry. Maps and charts very in size, from items of being held in one hand, to panels mounted on an entire wall. Maps are usually identified as to type of profation.

1.9.8. Motion Pictures

Motion pictures are available in many formats, libraries are usually involved with the 16-mm format standard 8-mm are now obsolete formats, Films are available with optical or magnetic sound tracks, with 16-mm films almost universally available on optical sound tracks only.

1.9.9. Pamphlets

The term pamphlets vary in definition among librarians, but it is generally an unbound work of one or more pieces of paper stapled together. Pamphlets usually provide information on topic of interest; they are not intended to be exhaustive in their contents, but to provide the reader with some specific information. Pamphlets very in size from small foldouts to stapled materials in a variety of sizes.

1.9.10. Periodicals

Periodicals are published on a regular or periodical basis, identified by title, and classified by volume, issue, and date. it may be paid a periodical has continuity. Incidentally, accumulated periodical can be bound, and many of then are available on microform.

1.9.11. Catalogues

Catalogues are mostly used as written form of communication. IT is a medium to dram the attention of the reader. It provides valuable information can use as substitute for the information in library. Catalogue may be issued in loose leaf or folder form.

1.9.12. Pictures

Pictures differ from maps and charts in that they are either photographs of objects or works of art drown or painted. Pictures are available as photographs, various kinds of graphics, and illustrations. A Librarian can inexpensively build a fine collection of pictures by clipping them out of discarded publications.

1.9.13. Programmed Instruction

Most programmed instruction currently being produced is being incorporated into computer programs. Programmed instruction includes materials designed to instruct the learner in a prescribed sequence of

- Stimulus
- Response
- Reinforcement.

1.9.14. Real Things and Models

Real things and models cover a multitude of materials and can very in size from very small to extremely large. Real things, also called realia. A model, on the other hand is a representation of a real thing that has been enlarged or reduced, a cutaway or cross- section simplified or modified for easier viewing or understanding, or ever a replica or blowup, miniaturization, or diorama.

1.9.15. Recording

1.9.15.1. Audiotape

Audiotapes are packaged in cassettes operating at standard speeds of 17/8 imps; cassettes operating at other speeds are for special applications. Recordings can be monaural stereophonic, of quadriphonic.

1.9.15.2. Disk

Disk recordings are available in various speeds or revolutions per minute(rpm). The current speeds still in production are 331/2 and 45 rpm. A new disc recording is the CD recording.

1.9.15.3. Video Tape

Video tape for libraries are generally available in the 1/2 inch VHS cassette format.

1.9.15.4. Video Disk

The laser video disk may eventually replace the video cassette as a means of storing video information. Presently, the video cassette can store more information than the laser disk.

1.9.16. Simultations and Games

Simulations and games are being packaged to provide the patron with a wide range of learning and recreational activities. They can be as simple as a printed scenario and as complex as boxes with playing boards, counters, disc spinning discs, etc.

1.9.17. Slides; Photographic

Slides differ from filmstrips in that they are individually mounted photographs and are not paced on one continual piece of film. In this way, can be rearranged, augmented, and deleted. Greatest use of slides occurs in the area of production of the visual arts.

1.9.18. Transparencies: Overhead

Overhead transparencies are used extensively in education and occupational training. They are usually mounted on 26-x30-cm(101/4x113/4inch) frames and contain a base transparency and possibly overlay transparencies[17].

There categories can, if needed be expanded or reduced, depending on the type of bibliography being prepared. The list can serve as a classification guide in categorizing media.

REFERENCES

1. Neilex, Robert. An are of innovation: the world electronics: 1930-2000, New York: McGH 1981, PP 192.

2. Seligman, L., A reading on the electronic book, an age of innovation: The world electronics: 1930-2000, New York: McGH, 1981. pp 200.
3. Lancaster, F.W., Towards paperless information system, New York: Academic, 1978. PP 1-4.
4. Ibid.,
5. Prasher, R.G., Information and its communication. New Delhi: Medallion, 1937. PP 13-14.
6. Rayudu, C.S., Media and communication, management, Bombay: Himalaya, 1993. PP 13-15.
7. Ibid.,
8. Khan, H,A., Communication media libraries and society. In: Sharma, C.D and Vyas, K., Developing horizons in library and information science, Vol. 2, Jaipur: Printwell, 1985. PP 180-181.
9. Panda, K.C and Gautam, J.N., In' fo Technology: On the cross'road: From ab'acus to Internet, Agra: Y.K, 1999. PP 1-2.
10. Sahai Shrinath., Library and the community, New Delhi: Today and Tomorrow's 1971. PP 177-179
11. Prytherch, J., Harrord's Librarians' Glossary of terms used in librarianship, documentation and the book crofts and reference book, 5th ed, Vermount: Gower, 1984. PP 403.
12. Satpathy, S.K and Rout, R.K., Impact of new media on collection development. PP 218.
13. Jagannathan, Neela., Media resources in academic libraries. In: Navalani and Trikha, S. eds., *Library and information services*, New Delhi: Rowat, 1999. PP 207-209.
14. Ibid.,
15. Kaula, P.N., Information and communication technology. In: *Impact and changes information technology in higher education, New* Delhi: Association of Indian Universities, 2000. PP 24-25.
16. Cabeceiras, J., The Multimedia Library: Materials selection and use, 3rd ED, New York: Academic, 1991. PP 19-23.
17. Ibid.,

2

Audio-Video and Microform Media

Primary, secondary and tertiary sources may not necessarily be printed on paper. Some of them may also come in audio-visual format such as films, tapes, videotapes, and gramophone records, electronic media.

2.1. AUDIO-VISUAL MATERIAL

Radio, Television, records, tapes, slides, movies, microforms, etc, have come in recent times. This development occurred in the last hundred or so years, yet these records of information are popular with people. Hence they are available both at home as well as in library and information centres. They capture the important events and moments of life. These records educate and entertain. A lot of educational material is being produced in this form. Copying such documents is easier, so their use is widening.

The word audio means sound or hearing, Visual means sight or the process of seeing a new sophisticated communication technology capable to visualize from it or to form a clear picture of some thing in a mind television, pictures, films etc; that are used as aids, to learning. Recent developments in audio-visual device are revolusioning communication media [1, 2, 3].

2.2 CATEGORIES OF AUDIO-VISUALS

	Mode		Media
1.	Audio	:	Phonorecords, tapes, radio broadcasts, etc.
2.	Visual	:	Epidiascope, over-head projector, etc. With transparencies, slides, etc.
3.	Audio-Visual	:	Film, TV, Video-tapes, tape slide presentations, multimedia package kits, with television, etc, and
4.	Computer and other electronic gadgets	:	Computer linked programmed learning use of telecommunication system in networking, etc. [4]

2.2.1. Video

The term video is often interchangeably used with television, although video is a medium that encompasses television and extends for beyond it. Video is both a production and distribution medium vehicle for art, entertainment and information.

Video entertainment through videocassettes has become popular in our society. Any sample survey will definitely bring out that most of the Videotapes of social, cultural, educational, and scientific interest are rare to get. Video is also one of the most effective media, which have entered in our libraries.

In the library TV/Video provide information and general answers as to how to read, i.e., show-how, do-how and know-how. In India UGC is providing special grant for the purchase of TV and Video to academic libraries, government and public libraries when concerned with individual library settings these media are of greatest advantages.

2.2.2. Video and Libraries

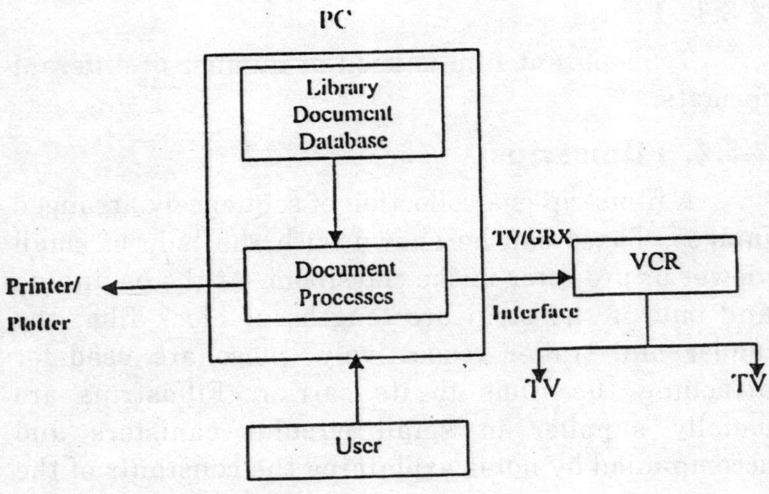

Fig. 2. Diagram for VCR usage for automated library services

Fig. 2, shows the significance if VCR usage for the library. As everybody Knows, the picture has much more impact than the word, and VCR can be used for having regular shows on varied topics like management, hitech information etc. Using intimation facility, library can provide the information regarding the video programme, from time to time through mail or past for the users [5].

2.3. AUDIO-VISUALS : PHYSICAL FORMATS

Over the last few years, there has been immense growth in the development of new technology, effecting the preparation, organization, storage and retrieval of information. Totally new concepts are appearing. These are revolutionizing the formats and equipments available and the prediction of these or their values is not possible. However, presently AV materials be put under following categories :

2.3.1. Films

Transparent film is used in number of different formats.

2.3.2. Filmstrips

A filmstrip is a collection of sequencely arranged images. These can be shown with the help of small viewer or projector in the classroom. At the beginning and end of the strip are lengths of block film, the lender and trailer respectively, these are used for attaching the films to its carrier. Filmstrips are usually supplier in small circular canisters and accompanied by notes explaining the constants of the pictures.

2.3.3. Cine Films

A cine film is sequence of images arranged vertically which gives appearance of movement when projected on to the screen at the correct speed. Again it is available is variety of formats.

a. **35 mm with sound track :** This format is almost exclusively used in public cinemas. A double sized frame (70 mm) is also in use.

b. **165 mm with optical sound track :** This is the common size used for educational purposes. The film should be projected at 24 frames per second. Film has sparockets on one side and sound strip on the other side.

c. **8 mm super/standard :** Normally, these comes in cartridges of 50 ft to 100 ft and can be easily screened in a small classroom for small audience with the help of portable projectors.

35 mm and 16 mm films are usually stored on open reels, each end of film with long blank piece of leader and trailer.

2.3.4. Magnetic Tapes

These can be further classified into two main divisions-sound and video.

2.3.5. Sound Tapes

These are commonly available in 3 formats open reel, cassette and cartridge. Tapes may also be separately glued to 16 mm and 8 mm Cine films to provide the base on which a sound track can be recorded.

2.3.5.1. Open Reel

commonly known as spool tapes this format is becoming increasingly uncommon for educational and classroom purposes but it is still widely used for the preparation and storage of masters or originals. Usual width or tape is 6.3 mm (1/4 inch). The tape is wound on reel with the magnetic surface on the inner side.

2.3.5.2. Sound Cassette

First developed by Philips during the 1960's is the most commonly used Audio device for educational purposes. The compact cassette has standard dimensions 4 inch X2½ inch and the tape is 0.15 inch (38 mm) wide. Magnetic coated surface is outside/ exposed. These Cassettes are run at the speed of 4.75 cm/Sec, or 17/8 inch/Sec for recording and playing purpose. The tape passes from one spool to the other actually remaining with the cassette.

2.3.5.3. Cartridge

This form of container is becoming less popular. The tape wound from the reel and back within the same box. Since the tape is continuous loop, it is not attached to the reel and has no leader tape and expensive equipment.

2.3.6. Video Tape

Almost all videotapes are now made with Chromium Oxide a major constituent of the magnetic coating. These are also available in open reel, cartridges and cassettes format. Open reel tapes are normally used for broadcasting purposes. Cartridges are basically an open reel within a box. Cassettes are enclosed system in which tapes wound from one reel to another, both with in the container. There are again available in various systems.

2.3.7. Plastic

Under this heading two formats can be considered.

2.3.7.1. Transparent Plastic

This material is for use with overhead projectors and is available in various thicknesses ranging from

Table 1. Various systems of video tapes

Name of system principal	*U-Matic*	*VHS*	*Beta Video*	*2000*
Manufacture	Sony	JVC	Sony	Philips
Maximum playing Time (mins)	60	240	215	480
Tape speed (cms)	9.5	2.34	1.87	2.44
Tape width (mm)	19.05	12.7	12.7	12.7
Container Dimensions (mm)	221 X 140 X32	188 X 104 X25	156 X 96 X 25	183 X 111 X 26

0.05 mm to 0.25 mm, either as single flat sheets or rolls.

2.3.7.2. Discs

Discs are marketed in 7 inch 10 inch and 12 inch diameter sizes, the central hole for the spindle being about 7.5 mm in diameter. Recording on discs are made at 331/3, 45 and 78 revolutions per minute.

2.3.7.3. Video discs

There are various types of Videodiscs being developed and manufactured by different companies. Different brands differ in types of grooves and styles used for the recording/ playing [6, 7].

2.4. USAGE OF VARIOUS FORMS OF VA MATERIALS

Different media are suitable for different works. Broadly there can be categorized in Table 2.

2.5. COMPONENTS OF AUDIO VISUAL AIDS

The following are the components of Audio Visual aids :

1. Television/video projection,
2. Computer system,
3. Audio tape recorder,
4. 35 mm Slides,
5. Over head projection,
6. Motion picture film and video, and
7. Tape slide projection [8].

2.6. MOBILE AUDIO/VISUAL MEDIA

Mobile audio/Visual Media, including cassettes and films have come into increasing use in development projects, because of their versatility, mobility and adoptability. Mobile media are specifically targeted

Table 2. Usage of various forms AV materials

S.No.	*Medium*	*Uses*	*Equipments*
1.	**Audio**		
1.1	Tapes	Lectures of experts group discussions interviews. Reminiscences of senior professionals committee work casa recordings story method in teaching	Tape Recorder Editing equipments
1.2	Radio Broadcast	Distance education promoting library use	
1.3	Phone recorders	Lectures Reminiscences Music and sound effects (When used with visual medium)	Record Players
2.	**Visual**		
2.1	Epidiascope	Projecting printed pages Diagrams and charts, title pages of books Facsimile of catalogue cards, etc.	Epidiascope
2.2	Over Head Transparencies	Substitute of black board in writing Indicate the structure of the Lecture for presenting words, lists, statistics, harts and diagrams	

2.3	Slides	Original photographs copies of material from books pictures, Captions and graphs	Side Projector with remote control, 3.5 mm SLR camera Electronic flash.
2.4	Films	Distance education, user education staff communication Local history/ library history, case-studies.	Film Projectors
2.5	Video tapes	Lectures coupled with demonstration Descriptions Locations recording plus. All uses of films	Video player TV receiver Video camera
2.6	Television	Distance education promoting library user Orientation.	TV Projectors
2.7	Tape-Slide Programmes	Computer programme on a specific topic student/user/staff training, self teaching programmes	Tape recorders Tape Slidesynchsniser Automatic slide projectors.
2.8.	Multimedia packages	Orientation programmes, workshops, user education etc.	

to local situations and are easily reproduced and distributed. They lend themselves well to discussion groups, investigation forums and to repetition, yet carry the credibility of the electronic media and the excitement and liveliness of oral communication [9].

2.7. AUDIO/VISUAL COMPUTER INSTRUCTION SYSTEMS

In following AV computer in education and training are achieved though deferent materials. They are :

2.7.1. The audio/visual computer aided tutor system

The Audio/Visual compute Aided Tutor (AVCAT) employs slides and audio recordings as the major instructional media with the student work station. In view of this, existing sequential tape/slide training material can easily be modified to operate with AVCAT.

2.7.2. The Computer Audio/Video Instruction System

Computer Audio/Video Instruction System (CAVIS) is a practical commercial example of this approach to instruction. The system provides a teaching facility that integrates the use of Videocassette pictures, text, videotext and animation and presents there on a single TV screen with supporting sound effects.

2.7.3. The Interactive Video Information system

The Interactive Video Information System (IVIS) Multimedia workstation consists of a keyword, high-resolution Color Cathode Ray Tube (CRT) display, a pair of headphones, a videodisc player and a microcomputer system.

2.7.4. Computer Guided Learning System

Computer Guided Learning System (CGLS) for customer training illustrates the use of an open learning arrangement in which standards attend a Guided Learning Center at times when it is most convenient for them to come.

2.7.5. Logo Learning System

Logo is essentially a special purpose, procedural, high level programming language. It originated from the Massachusetts Institute of Technology (MIT) in the 1960s. The language was developed for the specific purpose of making computers make sense to children. Logo seeks to develop cognitive and linguistic skills as children use the compute to draw a riches, solve puzzles, play games and generate music [10].

2.8. MICROFORM

Library is a growing organism. Books are continuously added. The increasing growth of information sources has become a challenge in the efficient management and service. The explosion of literature has further added to the problems of acquisition, storage and retrieval. How to meet these challenges and problems has always engaged the attention of library and information managers. In dealing with books and other conventional sources, problems of rising prices, procurement time lags, postage, storage and binding, dusting, preserving, etc., up keeping costs are being increasingly faced. Financial crunches add to these problems. However, the need to reproduce and permanently preserve documents of search value is on steady increase.

Microform, right from the stage of its inception has undergone considerable change. The wide variety of user needs have given rise to a number of different forms in which microphotograph is made, stored and used [11, 12]

2.8.1. Microform

The vocabulary of the modern library has been deluged with the prefix micro. Microforms are printed or visual information is photographically reduced in the film format. Microfilms are the best answer. Document supply centers book distribution centers and suppliers of information products have resorted to this technology and hence more and more information sources are now available in microfilms users not apathetic to microforms espouse the cause of microform technology and enthusiastically welcome microforms, when hard copy is an available. Libraries and information centers necessarily must switch over to microform technology in order to facilitate larger access.

Although the microform collection at present is solely limited to in library use, but with the availability of flat tube technology it will soon be possible for individuals to own their own portable inexpensive readers. According to Cabeceiras, microforms presently constitute most efficient form for storing printed information because of tremendous saving in both space and material. It is a media form that will be present for years to come; and although it will eventually be replaced by digitized information that can be stored in computer the microform is presently a media format capable of providing certain information more effectively and efficiently than any other format.

The essentially of computer assisted (car) microform system are :

(a) A camera system for filing the source document

(b) A microform retrieval unit.

(c) a computer system for indexing and addressing the document.

(d) A terminal interface to couple the reader and the computer system [13].

2.8.2. Microform Formatting and Selecting

2.8.2.1. Microfile

Microfilm on reels was one of the earliest microfilms. It is still a popular choice because large greatest of information can be stored in a very little space at very low cost. Microform, which provides a high measure of film integrity, is desirable where information is added continuously in sequence with a less frequent updation.

Microforms are normally in two sizes : 16 mm and 35 mm (width) 16 mm films as loused in cartridges and 35 mm in spools 16 mm films are used to flare large quantities of information when the information is in text form.

35 mm films are used for graphics, drawings, maps and newspapers. Cartridges function as convenient packing for rolls of microform. Date is filed in a sequenced form on microform to be viewed consecutively.

2.8.2.2. Microfiche

A Microfiche or fiche is a sheet of film containing

multiple micro images in a grid pattern. The size of a microfiche usually is 14.5 cm × 10 cm. A standard microfilm can accommodate 98 pages in x-y direction, x-> 14 and y->7.

It is usually contains identification information that can be read with naked eye. Information can be viewed at random on microfiche when compared to a microfilm where it is in a sequential order. Microfiche can be easily duplicated for mailing. Security or reference purposes. The reduction range is 18x to 48x. Enlargement/reduction is normally interpreted in terms of x is photographic jargon. 18x means reduction of the size of the original to 1/18 and 48x to 1/18.

Most computer output microfilm (COM) is on microfiche. Microfiche is a small rectangular film and is very efficiency using is libraries.

2.8.2.3. Ultra Fiche

Ultrafiche is the same as microfiche but with a higher reduction ratio of more than 90X, thus permitting thousands of images per fiche. Ultrafiche offers the advantage of storing more information in less space than a standard microfiche.

2.8.2.4. Jacket

The jacket is a plastic carrier with single or multiple sleeves or channels designed to accept strips of 16 mm of 35 mm film. Jackets project the microfilm and facilitate organization of materials. Images may be copied or read directly from the jacket without removing the film. Jackets can be visibly titled for quick, easy film reference.

2.8.2.5. Scroll System

the microfiche "scrolls" through with the "cur marks" on the film helping to locate the required fiche and the individual coordinates.

2.8.2.6. Micro-Opaque Cards

Similar to microfiche in configuration, micro opaques are as their name implies, images on opaque stock. Therefore may be stored on both sides. Unlike microfiche where transmitted light is used for blow back opaques use reflected light. This is primarily used for reading because this cannot be easily duplicated.

2.8.2.7. Video Micrographies

Information can be input the system either through a conventional camera system in the case of paper documents, or through COM reader, if the original documents are in machine-readable form.

2.8.3. Storage, Indexing and Retrival of Microforms

2.8.3.1. Storage or Microform Filing

Filing system for microform represent perhaps the most neglected area of microform activity. it seems that hardware manufacturers and microform suppliers tend to forget the storage problem, which will ensue for their customers. There are very few storage or filing equipment that are available tailored made for microform.

2.8.3.2. Indexing

It is often said that the microform publications are a different species and therefore need special and

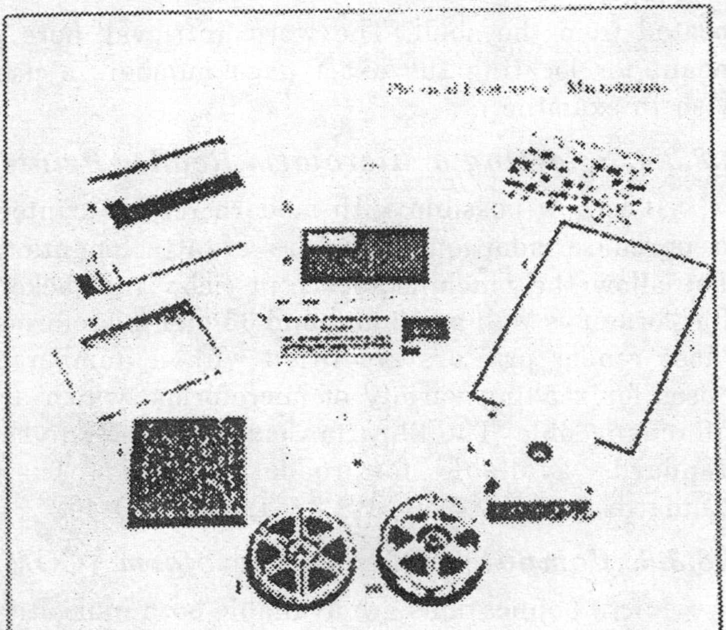

Fig. 3. Assorted microforms

of course different treatment. So far their physical format is concerned this is true, but so far as their technical processing or indexing is concerned individual bibliographic items in this format are amenable to the same rules as bibliographic items printed as a book.

2.8.3.3. Retrieval

Physical location of a document stored on microform is done the way a book or periodical is located from the shelf. The word 'retrieval' here is meant for locating the exact page numbers a user wish to examine.

2.8.3.4. Selecting a Microform Reader Printer

It is now possible with modern reader printers to purchase additional carriers of attachments is that allow the machine to accept fiche and jackets (flat forms) as well as 16 mm and 35 mm microforms. These reader printers are fitted with a number of lenses for reading variety of microforms, which are interchangeable. The librarian may also refer to the standards available for reader printers. These standards are: BS 4191; BS 3861; and ISO 452.

2.8.3.5. Computer Output Microform (COM)

Micro publications are available both in positive while users prefer positive, it is easier to get good prints from the negatives. Computer Technology (CT) and Reprographic and Micrographic Technology (RMT) have brought in their wake manuals in the book and library world. The personal computer (PC) has become a thing of the past. The CD-ROM, CDI and the later Hard Held Electronic Book (HHEB) gave a new meaning to the state of the art.

2.8.4. Setting up a Microfiling Unit

Libraries having documents of archival value will need to have their own microfilming unit. The equipments and infrastructure required for such unit is given bellow in brief.

1. Equipments :

   (a) **Camera** : Microfilm Camera (166 mm and 35 mm)

Microfiche Camera (step and repeat)

With a title camera for printing bold titles :

(b) **Processor** : Microfiche Processor,
Microfilm Processor;

(c) Microform Reader Printer and/or a continuous Reader Printer;

(d) Microfiche/film Duplicator;

(e) Other materials like chemicals, films, fiches, etc. [14, 15, 16, 17]

2.8.5. Categories of Micro Publications

Following types books macro publications are issued to cover the

1. Documents containing new information not previously published for sale or distribution these may be journals and books.
2. Re-issuing material simultaneously published in hard copy, e.g. newspapers.
3. Making single or multiple copies of proprietary information or of books and documents which cannot have large demand.
4. Rare out of print books and periodicals, etc.
5. Reference works.
6. Library catalogues.
7. Archival material and fragile manuscripts.
8. Data serener which need constant updating etc.

10. These and dissertations, which in a majority of cases do not get published [18].

2.8.6. Microform Production Standards

The three major committees responsible for microform standards are the Association for

Information and Image Management (AIIMA), the American National Standards Institute (ANSI), and the International Standardization Organization (ISO). These groups monitor and create the various specifications of microform software and hardware.

The type of film processing selected has to be considered. At present there are three acceptable standards:

* Silver halide
* Diaz, and
* Vesicular films.

2.8.6.1. Silver Halide

Silver Halide, the most durable of the three processes, is formed by converting silver halide crystals in the exposed are as to metallic silver during the exposure and developing process. As a result of the conventional processing, a black image is left with only the clear film based and gelatins remaining in the unexposed are as silver halide film is susceptible to oxidation blemishes call redox blemishes (fungal attack) in the gelatin and are easily scratched as the silver is fixed in emulsion.

2.8.6.2. Diazo Film

Diazo film is a slow print film, sensitized by means of diazonium salts. Its generally produces a non-reversible image (Positive produces Positive) when the salts are exposed to ultraviolet light. Diazo film in resistant to fungus and humidity, but is sensitive to light and heat. A problem occurs because these are several types of diazo films available, each with its own time-fade characteristics, and venders rarely, if even, indicate the particular Diazo process used.

2.8.6.3. Vesicular Film

Vesicular film has it slight sensitive element suspended in a plastic layer. When it is exposed, strain with in the layer forms a latent image. At present the most effective of vesicular films is Xidex XPPG, which is more resistant to heat than any other type of vesicular film. Vesicular film is generally unaffected by light, as the vesicles are fixed and not sensitive to light, including ultraviolet light [19].

2.8.7. Microfilm Applications

Microform finds various applications. Book trade uses microform for producing catalogues, lists of out of print books, indexes to books and nonbook materials. Universities in USA and UK publish their prospectus and admission material to distributed them free of cost to the students.

Engineering design, drawing etc., are invariably stored in microform as the originals are unwieldy to use. Storage of such drawings in their original form is a difficult task too. Organizations that collaborate on research projects make available materials mutually in microform so as to ensure their integrity and reliability. Newspaper offices and archives use microform technology for preserving their records. Original manuscripts, literature on palm leaves and prehistoric materials can be preserved permanently using microform technology. These applications are outside the purview of libraries and information centers.

2.8.8. Advantages

The benefits of going in for microforms in libraries for out weight the disadvantages which is why modern libraries send to go in more and more for this form :

1. The advantage of microforms is that they save space bulky newspapers and back volumes of journals, if put on microforms, can save space upto the extent of 28%.
2. Micro documents are more durable than paper documents. This way all documents are more durable than paper documents. This way all precious materials can be safely and easily preserved for posterity.
3. This form is this utter weightlessness, which would go a long way in effecting considerable savings in cost of construction of buildings.
4. Then again microforms are more expendable and replaceable than the book form.
5. Dissemination of information is much quicker with the microform. It is calculated that one fourth of the time taken together information from the book is required to obtain it from a microform.
6. The cost of processing the microform of the document would be 1/10th of its hard copy. The printing costs would be greatly reduced enabling smaller editions of 30 to 100 copies to be brought out without much risk.
7. The again, the microform holdings can be converted into electronic form. Therefore, it is certainly advantage to go in for a positive microform policy in the matter of acquiring documents for libraries.

2.8.9. Disadvantages

1. Microform is not user friendly. The user has to make special efforts to consult a book on microform. The tendency on the part of the user would be that he would go without consulting the document if it is in the microform unless the matter is important and urgent.
2. The reader has a feeling that second next option is being foisted on him. He thinks that the choice is not his but that of the librarian.
3. Microform lacks facilities. An ordinary book can be read anywhere at any time such as in the library, at home, in a restaurant or other similar places.
4. Reader resistance also arises from the fact that the system puts strain on the eyes and body.
5. There are other problems at tendendant on thids system dependent media, such as :
    1. The cumbersomeness of the reader
    2. Voltage fluctuations,
    3. Power breakdowns
    4. Non-availability of space parts
    5. Lack of servicing facilities.
    6. Environment, and
    7. Deflective in taking down notes.
6. Thesis and dissertations in a majority of cases do not get published [20, 21].

REFERENCES

1. Gupta, O.P., Audio-Visual Media for educational communication. **In**: ISAAC, D and Others. eds. *Academic libraries : Role in the national development*, Madras : T.R., 1993. PP 259-263.

2. Zorkoczy, Peter., Information Technology : A introduction, New Delhi : EWP, 1985. PP 71-73.
3. Navlani, K., Changing scene of information sources. **In** : Navlani, K., ed., *Library and information services,* New Delhi : Rawat, 1999, PP 73-75.
4. Guptha, K.P., and Pawan, U, eds., Library and information science : Current trends in India, Jaipur : RBSA, 1986. PP 36-37.
5. Kabir, S.H., Role of libraries and information centers in view of TV and video media. Herald of Library Science, Vol 35 (1-2), 1996. PP 31-34.
6. Chadha, R.K. and Arora, J., Audio-Visual materials in academic libraries. **In**: Rastogi, U.C. ed. *Changing dimensions in academic libraries,* Lucknow : Lucknow Christian college, 1989 PP 30-33.
7. Zorkoczy, Peter., **Op cit.**, Pp 71-75.
8. Sayeelakshmi, R., Information retrieval through Audio-Visual aids and multimedia. **In** : Satyanarayana, B.eds., *Multimedia : Its applications in library and information science,* Chennai, T.R., 1998. PP 175-180.
9. Raja, B.W.D., Different learning approaches in Multimedia computer. **In** : Association of Indian Universities., eds., *Information Technology in higher education,* New Delhi : AIU, 2000. PP 22-23.
10. Kaula, P.N., Information and communication technology impact and challenges. **In** : Association of Indian Universities., eds., *Information Technology in higher education,* New Delhi : AIU, 2000. PP 22-23.
11. Gill, N.S., Role of information technology in office automation. **In** : Association of Indian Universities., eds., *Information Technology in higher education,* New Delhi : AIU, 2000. PP 22-23.
12. Arora, J and Chadhua, R.K., Micrographic system : Guidelines for selection of microforms and equipments : **In** : Rastogi, U.C. ed., Changing dimensions in academic libraries, Lucknow : Lucknow Christian college, 1989. PP 44-53.
13. Cabeceiras, J., The multimedia library : Materials selection and use, 3rd, New York : Academic, 1991. PP 234-243.

14. Arora, J and Chadhua, R.K., **Op cit.** PP 44-53.
15. Reddy, M. Sankara., Microform technology in information storage and retrieval. **In** : Venugopal, M.V. and Others, eds., *Vistas in library, information systems and networks*, Agra : Y.K., 1999. PP 133-139.
16. Jain, M.K. : Library manual : A practical approach to management, Delhi : Shipra, 1999. PP 74-79.
17. Arora, J and Chadhua, R.K., **Op cit.**, PP 44-53.
18. Sign, S.P., Treads in information technology and its impact on dissemination of information, New Delhi : Rawat, 1999 PP 107-110.
19. Cabeceiras, J., **Op cit.,** Pp 234-243.
20. Zorkoczy, Peter., **Op cit.,** PP 71-75.
21. Reddy, M. Sankara., **Op cit.,** PP 132-139.

3

ELECTRONIC MEDIA

Information Technology (IT) is electronic technology used for collecting, storing, processing and communicating information. There are two main categories. Those, which process information (computer systems); and those, which disseminate information (such as telecommunication system). IT has a wider connotation for libraries, which include in addition technologies like repro-micrographic technology: technical communication technologies and database creation and use.

The term 'Information Technology' is widely used in UK, USA, and India 'Telemetric' is used for the same in France and 'Informetrics', is widely used in Russian and other socialist countries.

According to ILA Glossary Information Technology is " the application of the computers and other technologies to the acquisition, organization, storage, retrieval and dissemination of information" [1].

UNESCO defines IT "scientific technology used in engineering disciplines and the management techniques used in information handling and processing their application, computers and their interaction with men and materials and associated social, economic, and cultural materials]] [2].

IT is general meant a technology used for information disseminator, which includes systems like telex, fax, teleprinter, e-mail and so on. For a librarian, it has a much wider connotation, which includes the technologies and systems like microfilm, microfiche, CD-ROMs, computers, information networks, etc. In it, will discuss all those technologies, which libraries and information centers used for dissemination of recorded information.

3.1. INFORMATION TECHNOLOGY AS RELEVANT TO LIBRARIES

Information technologies that are relevant to libraries mainly cover the following :

(a) Computer Technology;

(b) Telecommunications Technologies;

(c) Reprographic Technologies;

(d) Library Technologies;

(e) Technical Communication.

The activities and services in libraries in which those technologies are used are indicated in Fig. 4.

The Information Technology Task Force recently constituted by the Government also seems to accept this wider connotation of IT, as can be seem from the recommendation it has made [3, 4].

3.2. APPLICATION OF INFORMATION TECHNOLOGY

Information Technology is useful for information handling and information processing. It is the fastest growing technology. Today it has surpassed all other

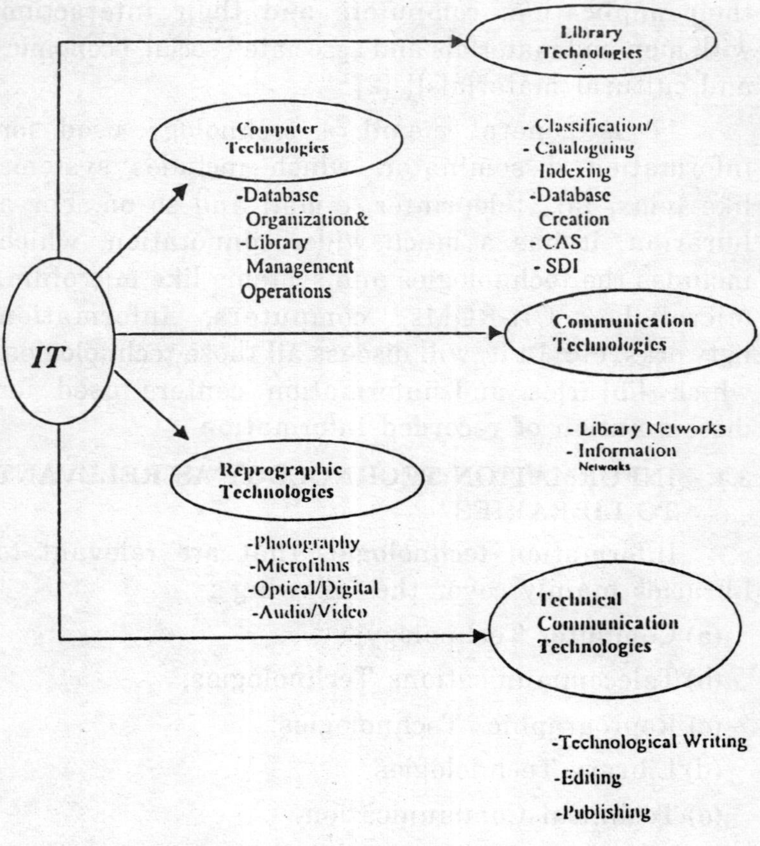

Fig. 4. Areas of Information Technology as relevant to libraries

technologies and it is playing a crucial role in the economic, industrial, social, scientific and technological development of the country. Its applications to library and information fields are becoming popular, because of complexities involved in information storage and retrieval. The basic concept of information technology is to make the librarians, information scientist, documentalists, etc., free from the traditional routine jobs. The aim of using information technology are enhancing efficiency, improving reliability and reducing costs.

3.2.1. Word Processor

Word processor is electronic equipment used for formatting and editing text or matter for storage in the memory of the equipment or an external storage facility like floppy disk for obtaining outputs repeatedly in desired manner.

3.2.2. Reprography

Development of reprography or duplicating technology made many things easier for libraries/ information centers as well as for users: The technological inventions are :

1. Photography
2. Photostat
3. Xerography

3.2.3. Micrography

This is one of the most important techniques used for information storage retrieval [5].

3.2.4. Computer

The history of computer dates backs to 5000 BC. When the calculating table called 'abacus] was designed by the Chinese to aid in calculations. Later Greeks and Romans also used it. This devices is still used in some parts of Middle East, far East, India and Chain ion schools for teaching mathematical calculations.

In 1617 John Napier, a Seotish mathematician published a work describing methods of performing the fundamental operations or multiplications and division of means of 'rods'.

The French scientist philosopher blaise Pascal constructed a digital calculating machine in 1642, which resembles a modern disc calculator.

A German Mathematician Gottfried van Leibniz invented a more advanced machine for purposes of addition in 1694. It was called 'Stepped Reckoner'.

Charles Babage of UK first conceived of the Lifference Engineers and 'Analytical Engine' in the early as 19th Century automatic devices to perform a sequence of operations.

However Aiken of Harvard University in association with IBM engines developed a fully automatic calculator called "Automatic Sequence Controlled Calculator in 1944".

The first truly Electronic computer was the "Electronic Numerical Integrator and Computer (ENIAC) designed by Mauchly and Eckert and completed at the University of Pennsylvania in 1946-47.

Computer is simply an electronic calculation machine, which consists of various parts such as input, output, memory, central unit and Arithmetic logic unit to perform various functions such as book section acquisition circulation etc. Computer two types of operations such as on line and offline.

Professor Saffady defined computer as "computer is widely and some what loosely used to denote a variety of information processing machine. Further the most descriptive term central processor" better suggests the computers role as the most functional component in information processing system" (saffady 1983).

Computer retains the basic characteristics of

acquisition policy like checking of collection, section ordering etc. But replaces paper processing manual work. If the library has an online catalogue or master acquisition file, it can be searched by computer to determine whether a given item as owned or not in computer acquisition system bibliographic information's are converted to machine-readable form entry into a master acquisition file [6].

3.2.4.1. Generation of Computers

Table 3. Generation of computers

Generation	*Period*	*Length of the period*	*Technology*
1st Generation	1946-60	About 15 years	Vacuum tubes
2nd Generation	1960-64	About 4 years	Transistors
3rd Generation	1965-70	About 6 years	Integrated Circuits
4th Generation	1971-85	About 15 years	Large Scale Integrated Circuits and very large Scale intimated circuits
5th Generation	1985-	Work is progress	Artificial Intelligence

3.2.4.2. Components of Computers

There are five basic units in a computer :

Table 4. Component of computers

Sr. No.	*Unit*	*Function*
1.	Input device	To receive data
2.	Output device	To produce results
3.	Arithmetic/Logical Unit	To perform arithmetic & logic functions
4.	Control Unit	To understand & execute instructions in a logical sequence
5.	Memory Unit	To hold data, instructions, processed results

3.2.5. Online Bibliographic Database

Database can be defined as a collection of machine-readable records, to be accessed through a computer. Online bibliographic database as a collection or records usually derived form machine-readable version of the principal abstracting and indexing journals held online in a rapid access computer store.

Bibliographic verification can be similarly automated by searching the shared cataloging databases. For instance, MARC LC/LINE databases are offered by the online search services.

R.R. Bowker company now offers its Book in Print database through the DIALOG and BRS online search service.

3.2.6. Videotext and Teletext

Videotext and teletext are tow important developments among the new information storage and displays technology. Videotext and View data are interactive system for transmitting text or graphics stored in computer database via the telephone network for display on a television screen. The videotext system is very useful for updating encyclopaedias works, dictionaries, financial information etc., and also for doing SDI bibliographic and document delivery and referral services.]

3.2.7. Teletext

BBC developed the system in 1972. The term teletext is a generic name for pseudo-interactive information retrieval system using a one-way telecommunication link to carry digital encoded textual, graphic or computer readable information.

3.2.8. Electronic mail and Message System (EMMS)

Electronic Mail is a message service using electronic and telecommunication to deliver hard and soft copy information.

The Electronic-Mail Network provides means for rapid information transfer among users. The messages are composed and sent to mailbox file using the computer and modern. The mail is left in the mailbox file on computer and users can view the mail anytime.

E-Mail and Message System helps in rapid transmission of information, short messages, actual figures etc. This reduces the staff time in processing Inter Library Lending requests. Others users of Electronic Mail are correspondence with users suppliers and other libraries, quick reference queries, teleconferencing etc. The E-Mail requires a telecommunication network for information transmission.

3.2.9. Telefacsimile

It is popularly know as FAX, which refers to the use of normal telephone line coupled to an electronic device commonly called FAX machine. The purpose of FAX is to send and receive copies of documents between two locations within minutes. It is the most sophistical electronic system for the delivery of Inter Library Loan (ILL) requests and documents transmission. It facilities an extremely rapid transmission of data. The most useful implication of this technology is the reduction of the turn around time' for ILL service to an absolute minimum.

3.2.10. Hypertext and Hypermedia

Hypertext allows to link together any textual information blocks whereas. Hypermedia provides non-lineal linking capabilities between heterogenous blocks of information such as text graphic, sound, animation etc., created with different application. These services allow deposit and continual revision of linked electronic documents and simultaneous access to a large collection of documents.

The commercial Hypertext available in the market is Apple Computer's HyperCard and Owl International guide for the IBMPC and Macintosh.

3.2.11.Compact Disc Read only Memory (CD-ROM)

This is the digital optical disc like a music disc, which can be produced, inexpensively in large qualities. CD-ROM is a read only medium.

3.2.12. Resource Sharing and Networking

Resource Sharing of resources among libraries otherwise know as Library Co-operation. The modern terminology given to Resource Sharing is called Networking.

In India various library Networking system functioning such as NICKET, INFLIBNET, INDONET, DENNET [7].

3.3. OTHER INFORMATION TECHNOLOGIES IN THE INDIA

During last five years Information technology (IT) has taken a new turn in order to make the human life not only informative but also easier and comfortable. owing to untried efforts of the Scientists and technocrats, several new technologies have been introduced into Indian Information Technology.

3.3.1. Voice-Mail

Voice-Mail technology is a sophisticated telecom service, which is somewhat identical to the mailbox system in post offices and would be a boon to those who do not have their own telephone or people who are regularly on the move for business. The first voice-mail in India was introduced by the Mahanagar Telephone Nigam Ltd. (MTNL) initially for the customers in Bombay and Delhi, which was inaugurated by former, Union Minister of state for communications.

3.3.2. Hybrid-mail Technology

The postal services in the country entered into a new phase of modernization with the introduction of 'Hybrid Mail' technology, involving electronic transmission of written material in English using computer terminals connected through satellite.

3.3.3. Multimedia Telephone Technology : ISDN

The Department of Telecommunications (DoT) introduced a new range of powerful communication services to both business and residential subscribes with the introduction of Integrated Services Digital Network (ISDN) in India since Oct 23, 1995.

3.3.4. Cellular Mobile Telephone Technology

Man have had never imagined carrying a pocket sized telephone and talking to any one at any time form any where round the globe but this dream become a reality with the introduction of cellular mobile phone system in the country in 1995.

3.3.5. Radio Paging Technology

Radio paging is a one-way communication service to alert a person who cannot be contacted over telephone. The modus operandi is for an individual to send a message to paging control room, which has been set up by AIR, over the PSTN telephone line. the message first gets encoded through the RSA paging encoder before it is fed to the transmitter either through a landline or a radio link.

3.3.6. Telecommunication

The rapid technological advancements in the field of telecommunication call for constant up gradation of technology. As an effort in this direction, 75% of the Elctro-Mechanical Telephone Exchanges have been replaced by modern Electronic and Digital ones. Several value-added services like Radio paging Cellular Mobile telephone, Electronic mail Voice mail including Audio text and satellite services have been to introduced the era of advanced technology [8].

3.3.7. Barcode technology

Barcode is not a new technology as many of us would think. It has been around since the late 1940s and saw it's first commercial use in 1940 as a method for tracking railroad cars. Since then, this automatic method of identification has been found wide acceptance in the grocery and materials handling industries.

A number of possibilities exist for using barcode. One such possibility is its use in libraries. The Kentish town branch of CAMDEN Public Library was the first library to use the plessey Light Pen System in 1972. A U.K. firm, SB Electronic Systems, has a barcoded label. Another method of bar-coding, known as Codabar, is used by Geac in library circulation system. The University of Surrey library uses a bar coding method Known as 2 of 5 and these labels are 'read' by microprocessor based light pen terminals. Many American libraries use Code-48, which includes alphabetic characters.

3.3.7.1. What is Barcode

Barcode can be defined as a self-contained message with information encoded in a series of block bars of varying breadths and white spaces between every two of them. The bars and spaces represent a series. of characters or digits. These are readable only by a scanner, which sends messages to the computer that detoxifies the number of the digits. The computer identifies such bars as '0's and '1's representing characters or digits in such a form as can be identified by computers only.

3.3.7.2. Code and Symbology

A decode is the combination of numbers and characters that represents an entity, such as a part number. The symbology is the language used to represent the code in Machine Readable Form. The spaces of varying width is called the barcode symbol.

3.3.7.3. Symbology for Library Applications

There are many symbologies for barcodes. In fact, there are more than fifty different coding schemes with five of them being in common usage i.e., (1) European Article Numbering (EAN); (2) Universal Product Code (UPC); (3) Interleved 2 of 5

(4) codebar; and (5) code-39. The first three are only number. There is a facility in Codebar to enclose $, -, :, +, % in addition to numbers.

Code-39 also known as code 3 to 9, is alpha and numeric. The code is of any length and all the capital letters of the alphabets as well as numerics and the additional characters of '$' '-' ':' '.' '?' '.' '+' '%' and 'space' can be enclosed. Lower case letter can not be enclosed. Code 39 is always started and ended with an asterisk (*), known as the start/stop character and may be used only at the beginning and end of the code. In code 39, bars and spaces are used to encode an individual characters is represented by 5 bars and 4 spaces. Three of these elements are wide and six are narrow. 43, which is bi-directional. This means that whether an operator scans a barcode form left to right or right to left, the reader can interpret the symbol and transmit the data in proper sequence.

Today computers are alpha-numeric, an as a part of basic computer technology, barcodes also should be alpha-numeric. Code 39 is alpha-numeric whereas the other codes are numeric. This feature has been the dominant consideration in its adoption by libraries and by several major industrial segments. Among symbology codes, available with the Space Applications Centre (SAC) library software for generating labels, code-39 has been configured.

3.3.7.4. Basic Requirements for Barcode Applicaiton

The following are the basic requirements for implecating barcodes in library applications. Complete barcode system plan at Space Applications (SAC) library is given in Fig. 5. The hardware and software required for the purpose are :

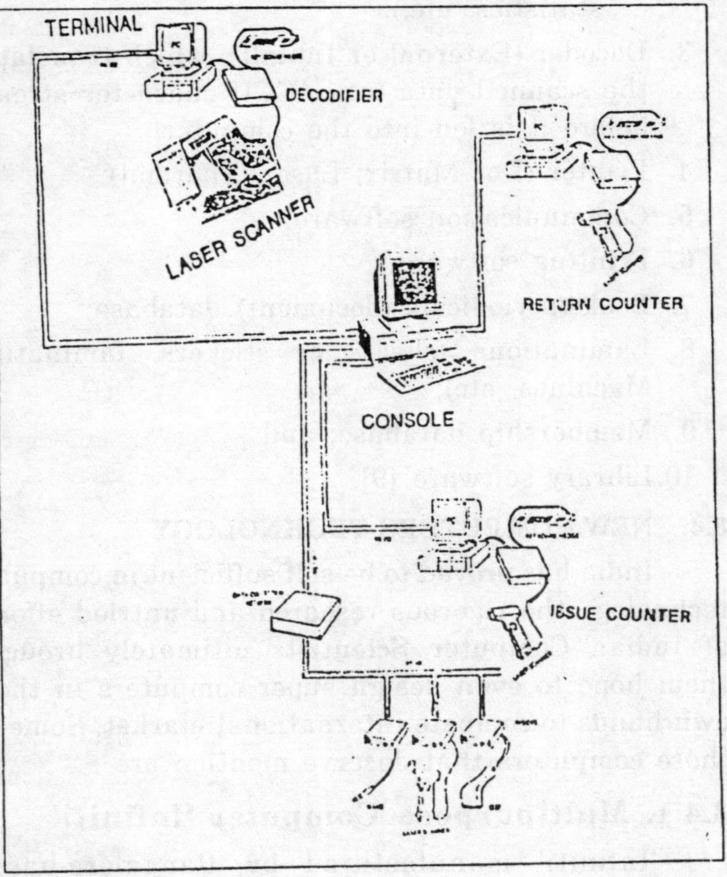

Fig. 5. Complete barcode system plan at SAC library

1. Personal Compares (IBM compatible);
2. Barcode Scanner to read the barcode labels, which can be a contact or non-contact type;

a. On-line Scanner (connected with computer for issue/rectum process);

b. Off-line Scanner (useful when there is no light and also for physical verification, user statistics, etc.);

3. Decoder (External or Inbuilt), which translates the scanned data into ASCII character stream before it is fed into the computer;
4. Printer (Dot Matrix, Laser, Thermal);
5. Communication software;
6. Printing software;
7. Books/periodicals (document) database;
8. Laminations (sheets or stickers, laminating Machines, etc);
9. Membership database; and
10. Library software [9].

3.4. NEW COMPUTERS TECHNOLOGY

India has proved to be self sufficient in computer technology the rigorous research and untried efforts of Indian Computer Scientists ultimately brought them hope to even design super computers in their own hands to compete international market. Some of those computers that deserve mention are :

3.4.1. Multipurpose Computer 'Infiniti'

'Infiniti' manufactured by Bangalore-based Cerebra Integrated Technologies Ltd. (CITL) is the country's first multipurpose all in one home computer, which can work as a TV, a CD player, an FM radio, a stereo amplifier with karaoke and server as a fax, has been launched in Banglore in oct. 1995.

3.4.2. Parallel Processing Computer 'Pace-Plus]

Six years after plugging into the race to develop super computers, deface scientists in Hyderabad could succeed in bringing the country's fastest parallel processing computer, 'PACE-PLUS' (i.e., Processor for Aerodynamic computation and Evaluation Plus (PACE+).

3.4.3. Multimedia PC: 'Presario CDS 520'

A new MM personal computer, which can act as a CD (compact disc) system, phone enters, fax center, and TV, has entered Indian market in 1995. This PC modelled Presario 'CDS 520', comes from Compaq of the US, with a 486-5x2 processor and 420 Mb hard RAM is expendable to 64 Mb selecting TV channel or playing a MM CD or sending a fax is achieved by a user friendly software. It's phone centre has an answering machine which has 10 private voice-mail boxes with remote access. it can also send and receive faxes or connect to communication links such as e-mail or internet. It comes with a software library containing MS Encarta (Encyclopedia), MS works, and MS-DOS 6.2. The system comes with 12 CDs and TV turner. It s being marketed in India by Tangerine Electronic System Pvt. Ltd. [10].

3.5. ELECTRONIC LIBRARY

The Electronic Library is a store house of information, documents, audio-visual and graphic materials stored in a variety, media ranging from printed books, periodicals, posters, and reports microfilms slides films, videos audio disks audio tapes, optical discs magnetic tapes, floppy disc etc. Electronic Library of the future is likely to be part of a network. In there, it is only necessary for one Electronic copy of a document to be stored in the whole world. A wold Electronic Library would be a possibility.

Electronic Library deals with both house keeping operation Online Public Access Catalogue (OPAC) and the generation of management information and information retrieval systems like external databases and associated series and products and internal or local databases and their associated services and products. The associated services include current Awareness Services (CAS), Selective Dissemination Information (SDI) etc.

The recent advances in computers and telecommunications have provided facilities to the extent that the users need not travel distances to visit libraries and they can have all what they want from a library at their working desk through their computer and telephone line. The Electronic Library makes available its enter catalogue and all information access tools in the form of database searchable on-line from the desk top PC. Once the required document is identified, the user may search for the document in a given CD-ROM through a CD-Net, which can be loaded in CD-Drive by an electronic mechanism of a juke-box. The juke-box may contain several hundreds of CD-ROMs and any one of them can be commanded for loading in a drive. The digitalized full text data from the CD-ROM start flowing through the wire to the screen. The whole documentation can be read on the scree; can be stored on the disc/floppy or a hard copy can be printed through a printer for reading at leisure.

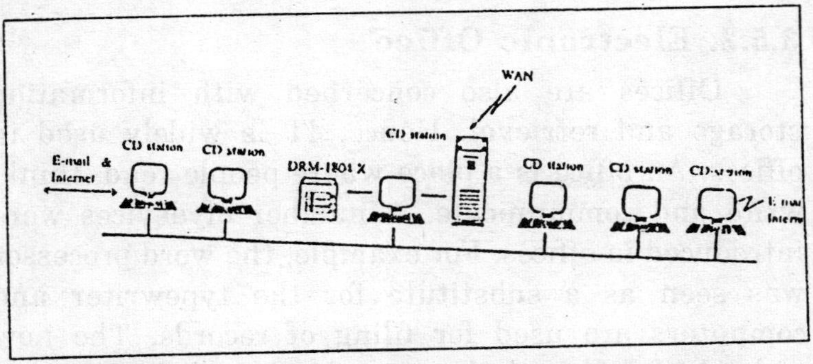

Fig. 6. Schematic view of Electronic Library

3.5.1. Role of Librarians

The present libraries are selecting, acquiring and organizing the print collections and are providing instructions and assistance in finding information within the collections. Electronic libraries are being built along similar self-service lines. They are designed for use with librarians serving not as intermediaries but as consultants. The librarian will continue to play the role of information provider to users in the electronic library system [11].

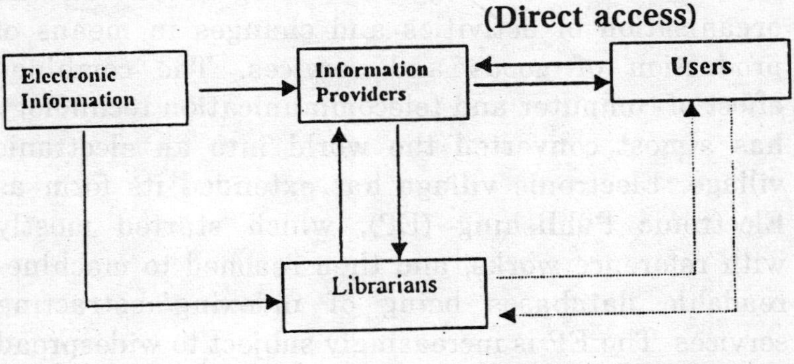

Fig. 7. Role of librarians in the Electronic Libraries

3.5.2. Electronic Office

Offices are also concerned with information storage and retrieval. Hence, IT is widely used in offices. An office is a place where people read, think, write and communicate. A number of devices were introduced in offices. For example, the word processor was seen as a substitute for the typewriter and computers are used for filing of records. The new technology affected the organization and nature of work in officer new technology has freed office work from its focus on the flow of paper between people and allowed the focus of activities to shift to the transaction recorded in the computers and the people making decisions and performing various tasks. It enabled faster decision making, elimination of redundant work and better utilization of human resources [12].

3.5.3. Electronic Publishing

Necessity is the mother of invention. Customer's demands are the biggest driving force for the organisation of activities and changes in means of production of goods and services. The combined effect of computer and telecommunication technology has almost converted the world into an electronic village. Electronic village has extended its form as Electronic Publishing (EP), which started mostly with reference works, and then reached to machine-readable databases being of indexing/abstracting services. The EP is increasingly subject to widespread usage of publishers of scholarly, academic and reference works from almost all fields of human knowledge.

Rapidly increase in the price of many printed scholarly journals and the general improvement in the technological in structure, are some of the many reasons for the emergence of EP. Thus leading to a situation whereby certain journals are published only in the form digital media.

Lancaster defined EP as, a publication process where the manuscripts are submitted in electronic format, edited, printed, and even distributed to readers (users) in electronic form by employing computers and telecommunication technology. The published information is distributed on state-of-th-at medium CD-ROMs, networks (on-line Internet, ISDN) etc. [13].

3.5.3.1. Electronic Journal

Electronic serials may be defined very broadly as any journal, magazine, e'zine, webzine, newsletter or type of electronic serial publication, which is available over the Internet. Within this broad definition, the titles can be electronically accessed using different technologies such as the World Wide Web (WWW), gopher, ftp, telnet, e-mail or listserv [14].

3.5.3.2. Need for EL-Serial Crisis

* Need to support paper and electronic methods of knowledge dissemination parallely.
* Information needed by faculty and students is increasing exponentially in the sciences.
* Interdisplinary research/new fields of research have increased the scientist's need for new information.
* Rising cost of journal publications coupled with the explosive growth in research and the concomitant explosion of paper journals in various disciplines have made it impossible for most

libraries to maintain a comprehensive selection of literature [15].

3.5.3.3. Role of librarian or Information Professional

Cybermetic theme of the librarian is to serve the society by meet the needs of the users of an information system/library with extensive use of the present technologies. However, the emergence of Internet and electronic publishing continue to widen the role of librarians. Librarian, acting as a custodian of information has gone through a dramatic change and from providing documents to his clientele, has switched to be an information provider, thus implying a shift in emphasis from a caretaker to a person who provides physical access to the collection.

The role of the librarian as a navigator has intensified in magnitude eventually leading to a greater orientation towards sound a video. In this context it is not easy for the librarian to learn and keep himself up to date with the latest technological advancements made in his professional area of work, more precisely, the knowledge and skill acquired today is next to obsolete tomorrow.

3.5.3.4. Issues and Concerns of Electronic Publishing

The problems and concerns of publishers, library and information centres as well as subscribers include issue of single articles versus full issues of EJ, copyright, users friendliness, pricing., intellectual property rights, professional role, networks, incompatible hardware and software, formatting graphics, scholarly recognition and obsolescence. The problems of creditability, accessibility, permanence etc. are follows :

* Accessibility;
* Acceptability;
* Display Incompatibilities;
* Intellectual Ownership;
* Copyright and Pricing;
* Preservation and Conservation;
* Standardization;
* Credibility;
* Permanence;
* Technical issues.

3.5.3.5. *Advantages*

The advantages of electronic publishing are:

* Maintenance of updating information
* On demand publishing;
* Information retrieval Just-in-time;
* Speed;
* Distribution;
* Retrieval;
* Multiple access;
* Manageability.

3.5.3.6. *Problems*

Some of the problems in electronic publishing are:

* High initial cost;
* Incompatible Hardware and Software;
* Weak infrastructure of Computer and Communication Network;

* Gar between Development and Develop Countries;
* Inreadability;
* Inconvenient to use;
* Delay in release;
* User Training [16, 17].

3.6. ELECTRONIC MEDIA

The latest format to enter into arena is electronic. It is usually used with a computer system or in association with a telecommunication system and covers magnetic, optical and magnetic optical media.

Libraries having only print materials are restricted and useful only to functional literates. They appeal to only one of the five senses, namely the sight of man. 'Sight' is a very powerful sense of man reading books makes highly inefficient by under-utilization of this sense by requiring it to scan linearly printed black alphabets of a language against white background of paper. Imparting knowledge has necessarily to make use of all the five senses of man and break the monotony of alphabets.

Electronic medium is a powerful tool having vast and wide applications in society. How much of it can be taken to their fold by library is left to one's imagination. Electronic medium emphasized effective use of the 'Sight' and 'heaving' senses and naturally rare use of the other senses.

3.6.1. Electronic Media Genius

Electronic media has pivotal role in information transfer, education culture, environment, health, polities, commerce, etc. The entertainment value of the media has overshadowed the informational, educational and cultural values. As a double-edged took of 'third wave' electronic media is encroaching and evading the readership of already under-used print medium. Electronic media coupled with advances in telecommunication make it economical to cover vast geographical area and almost complete population under information services.

Information technology and computer based systems are now dominating and revolutionizing libraries with versatility of their compact multimedia storage, electronic viewing and manipulation, instantaneous transfer and movement of information and inexpensive duplication. Print on paper is only one of the media for carrying information Electronic libraries expand the horizon of information gathering, increase perception, processing, comprehension and understanding of information by users through the compactly, concisely, less ambiguously and directly stored, information and provide for interaction with media as well as manipulation of information.

3.6.2. The characteristics of Electronic Media

The characteristics of electronic documents of information differ greatly form those of paper documents :

* Electronic documents are not localized. In other words, with the help of telecommunications connection they cal be used form any where with the user even not knowing where it is stored geographically.
* Several people can use online electronic media at the same time.
* It is easier to copy them or down load them in user file.

* They are less bulky. than the paper documents. New research is increasing their compactness.]
* They ar very flexible, as it becomes easier to revise, rearrange, reformat and combine them with other documents.
* When the material is highly changeable e.g., stock market price, train/aeroplane seledules, exchange rater of currency, it is easier to up date them.
* When manipulation of material is required, such as in a bibliography, which can be arranged alphabetically, or chronologically, subjectivise, etc. it educes work of arrangement.
* When scanning of names/words/phrases is desired such as in preparing concordance, or statistical analysis of words/ phrases is needed for linguistic research, etc. Electronic form is very useful as it does this work very easily and fast.
* When rapid communication of information is desired e.g., military/weather information this format is very useful.
* When material is required at remote places, where it is not available, this form helps in reaching them easily.

Electronic documents and new possibilities for use of texts, in this regard constituted enhancement of their use that is valuable in its own right [18].

3.6.3. Sources of Electronic Media

Many revolutionary changes are taking in telecommunication and information technology. The electronic media in general and the optical media in particular is replacing the print media. A paper less society, which was a distant image three decades lack, is a partial reality today; teletext, E-mail, voice-mail-multimedia and CD-ROMs are being used n all parts of the world. The newer media is making its presence in all types of libraries converting them as active provides of information.

Dr. S.R. Ranganathan classified documents into four categories, viz:

1. Conventional documents;
2. Neo-conventional documents;
3. Non-conventional documents;
4. Meta-conventional documents.

Categories of documents constitute largely the electronic sources of information, 'information explosion' made it essential to compress the information and transmit it faster. Technological developments in printing and communication brought into existence a variety of electronic media making the world a Global Village. These are available in formats such as discs, tapes, phonorecords, microforms, fax, e-mail, voice-mail, CD-ROMs, videotexts, Video cassettes, etc. The volume of the electronic source of information in on ascent for the last one quarter of a century [19, 20]

3.6.4. Electronic newspaper

The electronic newspaper is already a reality in the United States of America. Which brings the electronic information to the very doorsteps of the subscriber? The Columbia dispatch become the first newspaper is US to electronic on first July 1980 by making almost full of its educational product available to the house and business computer subscribers.

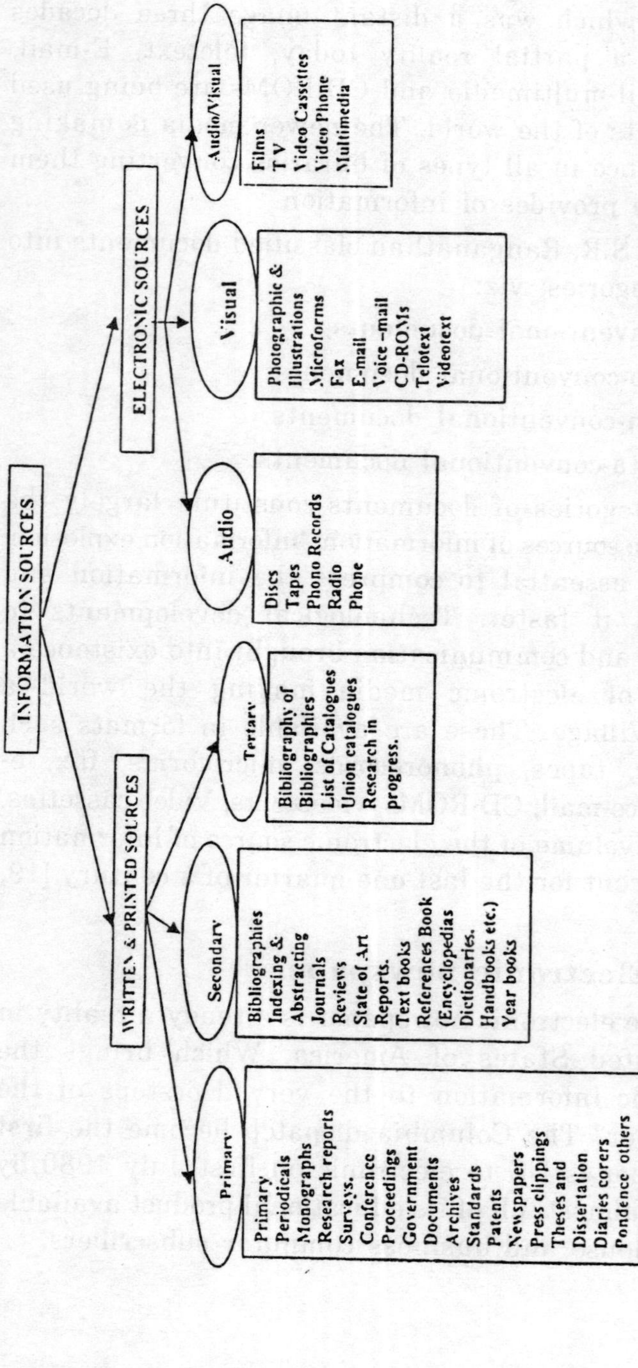

Fig. 8. Kinds of the written, The printed and the Electronic Source of Information

The subscriber have a television terminal in his home connected to the newspaper office through telephone lines. They cal 1 it 'cable TV' when the subscriber deals the newspaper office and turns on the video terminal, the latest edition of the newspaper of the newspaper like sports, entertainment. Market reports retail shopping, etc.

3.6.5. Electronic Media Saves Space

In the context where more and more documents are being published in paper form, libraries archives and information centres are facing an active shortage of space. Situations such as storing back documents under far from ideal conditions could lead to their physical damage. The problem could be considerably overcome by inverting older and less used documents into electronic media, (such as the CD-ROM). In this way, an entire stack of printed volumes could be accommodated in far lesses spaces than physical storage. This is not to claim that this method will store a document infinitely, for electronic media also suffers from mortality, but documents on this media can be effortlessly duplicated.

3.6.6. Electronic Media and Retrieval Efficiency

The utility of a document published on electronic media can be greatly enhanced as compared to its print version. This enhancement is coupled with reference to its retrieval features, embedded in its new form. A print document can have a contents page and a comprehensive index as its instruments of retrieval. On the other hand, if the full text of a document can be split into its constituent components, it could be built like a database and that could greatly augment the retrieval features of the document.

3.6.7. Electronic Media Demures Environmental Hazards

Paper is a forest-based product, and for paper, making widespread deforestation is followed. 'Save Paper' movements are called upon to check indiscriminate destruction of trees, so as to preserve and save the already degraded environment, Perhaps, now the time has come to switch over to electronic media to reduce our dependence on paper and help save the environment [21, 22].

3.7. NEW MEDIA

According to Dimities Anastassiou of Columbia University, two major technological developments will revolutionize the was information is created, processed and distributed in the coming decode. They are the gradual implementation of the National Information Infrastructure, and full digitization of all information service. As a result not only professionals but also individual users will be empowered will several unprecedented capacities to access, digital information from a variety of source including large Multimedia databases around the globe.

There is an evolving shared vision of the 'New Information' World. It is defined as a world of ubiquitous, reasonably priced digital information in any and all media available to everyone from a computer, TV, Palm, or wrist, as predictable, ordinary and universal as a toaster.

Technology has created a community of

approaches, which is assumed to have lead, into the convergence, even across what has traditionally been a strongly marked boundary. Experts feel that the adaptation of new technologies as a universal tool of information storage and retrieval has made it difficult and perhaps fulfill to attempt a fence around the information profession. This new media as represented in Fig. 9 is the means of representation and communication of inhumation using the forthcoming digital infrastructure. it allows interactive, multipoint communication in which computer; telecom and media (including libraries) tend to be integrated. This convergence is obviously catalyzed by the advancements is Imaging Science and Technology (IST) [23].

REFERENCES

1. Enser, P.G.B., information Technology and the libraries. *Library Science with slant to documentation,* Vol. 25(1), March, 1998. PP 1.
2. Patil, D.B. and Koogunurmath, M.M. eds., Library and information science, New Delhi : S. Chand, 1998. PP 5.
3. Kumar, P.S.G., fundamentals of information science, New Delhi; S. Chand, 1998, PP 3-5.
4. Murty, S.S., Role of librarians in the new millennium of information technology. *DESIDOC Bulletin of Information Technology,* Vol. 19 (4&5), 1999. PP 3-5.
5. Kasirao, V and Babu, R.B., Information technology i storage and retrieval. **In** : Satyanarayana, B., and Others., eds., *Information Technology : Issues and trends,* Vol. 1, New Delhi : COSMS, 1998. PP 3-8.
6. Kumar, P.S.G., **Op cit.**, PP 203-206.
7. Satpathy, S.K. and Rout, R.K., Impact of new media on collection development. **In** : Chopra, eds., *Library science and its facts,* Vol. 1, New Delhi : Ess Ess, 1998. PP 217-213.
8. Panda, K.C. and Gautam, J.N., In'fo technology on the

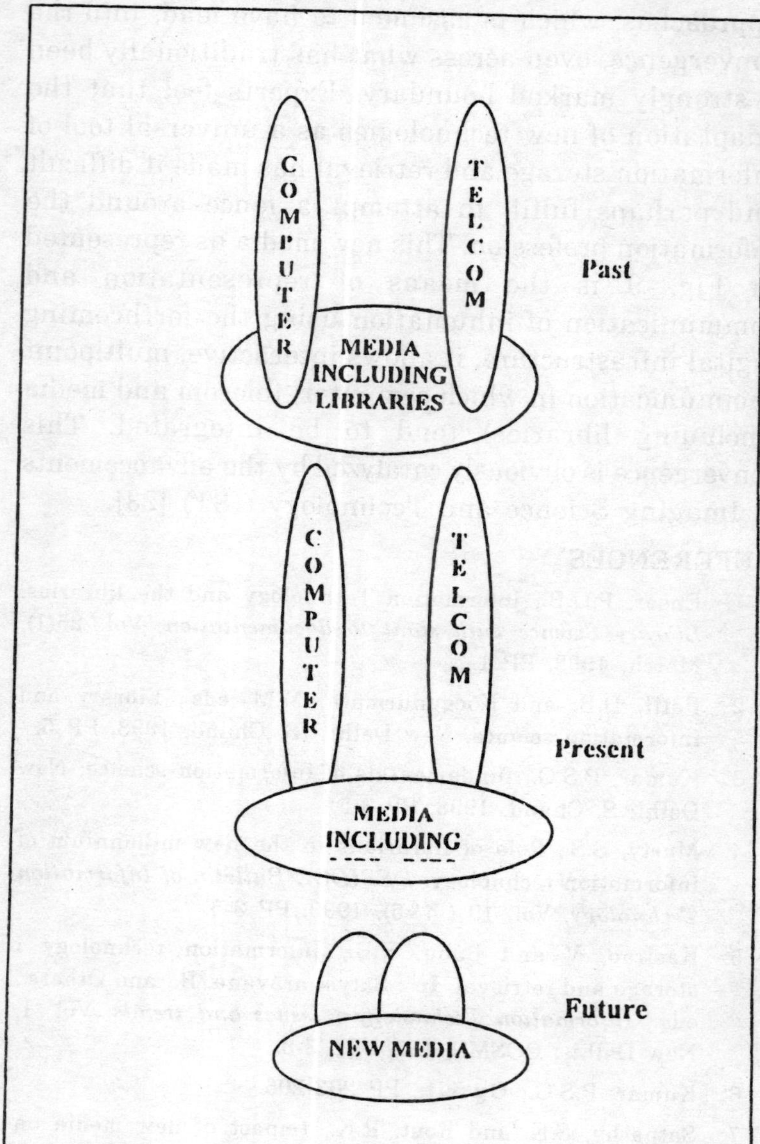

Fig. 9. New Media in the future Digital information Infrastructure

cross road : From AB'acus to Internet, Agra : Y.K. 1999 PP 5-10.

9. Patil, D.R., barcode system in libraries : Its uses and importance. *Annals of Library Science and Documentation*, Vol. 43(1), 1990. PP 1-5.

10. Panda, K.C. and Gautam, J.N., **Op cit.**, PP 201-303.

11. Dhaka, R.P.S. and Arora, K., Electronic Library : A mythor a reality. *Annals of Library Science and Documentation*, Vol. 42(4). December, 1995. PP 152-159.

12. Kumar, P.S.G., **Op cit.**, PP 203-206.

13. Lancaster, F.W., electronic publishing. Library trends, 37(3), 1987. PP 316-325.

14. http://www.coalliance.org/ejournal/what is.html.

15. http://sunsite.berkelery.edu/UCDL/reprt.html.

16. Moorthy, A.L. and Karisiddappa., Electronic Publishing : Impact and implications on library and information centers. **In** : Malwad, N.M. and Other., *Digital libraries : Dynamic store house of digitized information*, New Delhi : New age international, 1996. PP 15-29.

17. Gulati, A.N., Implications of electronic publishing on library and information centers. *Annals of Library Science and Documentation*, Vol. 46(4), 1996. PP 121-123.

18. Sridhar, M.S., Beware of electronic libraries/media. PP 243-238.

19. Ramaiah, L.S., Library and Information science in India : Glimpses and reflections, New Delhi : Ess Ess, 1996. PP 5-7.

20. Ramaiah, L.S., Images and perceptions in library and information science, New Delhi : Ess Ess, 1998. PP 168-169.

21. Battacharyya, M., Electronic publishing : The function of the new information society. **In** : FID., eds., Towards the new information society of tomorrow : *Innovations, challenges and impact*, Jaipur : 49th FID, conference and congress 11-17 Oct, 1998. PP 107-112.

22. Navalani, K., Changing science of information sources. **In**

: Navalani, K and Sudha, T., ed., *Library and Information services*, New Delhi : Rawat, 1999. Pp 77-79.

23. Prakash, B.P., Digital imaging : Technology trends and impact on libraries. **In** : Malwad, N.M. and Others., *Digital libraries : Dynamic store house of digitized information*, New Delhi : New Age International, 1996. PP 15-29.

4

STORAGE MEDIA

A number of storage media are available in the market for a long time. Libraries have been using microfilm, microfiche and ultra-fiche that help to store large volumes of data in a comparatively lesser space that the print media. In recent times, computer-based storage technologies have been developed to address information storage and retrieval problems faced by libraries and librarians. Broadly, computer storage technologies can be ground into magnetic and non-magnetic (optical) technologies. This paper overviews briefly the various magnetic and optical storage media having application in the library environment.

4.1. MAGNETIC STORAGE MEDIA

The magnetic storage devices came into the scene simultaneously with the arrival of microcomputers during the early 1980s. These include the primary storage hard discs/drives and the secondary (or auxiliary, removable) floppy discs. Their capacities have changed with the advances in technology. There are a variety of magnetic storage media available for the users to choose. These include : magnetic drum, magnetic and cartridge tapes (both analogues), digital audiotapes (Dates), floppy discs, magneto-optical discs and removable hard discs.

4.1.1. Magnetic Disc

Magnetic discs replaced the magnetic drums during 1956-57. RAMAAC 305, the first hard disc introduced by IBM, use 50 numbers of two-feet diameter discs to store 5 MB. During 1970s, several advances in the field resulted in discs of larger capacities, higher capabilities and lower costs. Removable disc packs/dirves are also used for large volumes of data. Later, the non-removable Winchester technology overtook the removable disc packs. The microcomputer started with 5 MB hard disc drives in 1980; it reached 2.5 GB in 1996. Since 1950s, the average capacity of a new computer's memory has grown 30 per cent mainly to facilitate storing more data. Since 1991, the capacity of the magnetic hard disc drives in the best of the PCs has accelerated to 60 per cent; it has moved from a few MB to a few GB. hard disc devices have faster access time (10-80 ms) and can hold several gigabytes of data.

4.1.2. Magnetic Tape

Magnetic tape is a sequential access storage medium. It is the slowest mass storage technology currently in use and is one of the cheapest storage media. The low cost per bit of stored data and large capacity makes it a popular archival medium. The recording medium is a thin polyester tape between 0.38 and 2.54 cm wide, about 0.25 mm thick and coated with magnetic particles. The 0.5-inch, 2,400-feet (730m) tape ha been the industry standard since it was first introduced commercially in 1953. The 9-track magnetic tape at 6,250 bpi has a capacity to hold one billion bits of data depending upon block and record sizes. It records data at 9 bits per frame, although 18-track (18 bits per frame) high density cartridge tapes fully enclosed in 5 × 4 × 1-inch cartridge boxes are also available.

Magnetic tapes and cartridges are used to store very large amounts of data that will not be used frequently. In a library environment, magnetic tapes can be used not take backup of files/databases, online public access catalogue, in house developed software, backup of archival files like circulation and acquisition data. These may also be used for exchange of large databases between libraries. A comparison of parameters of different magnetic tapes is provided in Table 5.

4.1.3. Cartridge Tape

After CD-ROM drives, cassette and cartridge tapes are the most frequently used devices with minicomputers and PCs. These have undergone many evolutionary changes. The 0.25-inch cartridge tapes are widely used with workstations, usually to take backup of large database/files. These can store up to 5 GB of data. Of late, 4-mm and 8-mm videotapes are also being used. These are low-cost and have longer access time than the floppy discs. A typical tape cassette can hold up to 50 MB of data with density range of 6,400-10,000 bpi. In contrast, a mainframe cartridge can store at 38,000 bpi and a 550-feet tape cartridge can hold one GB data, the same amount as the 2400-feet, 0.5-inch tape. Cartridges (of the same size) with shorter length hold less data; but they are

Table 5. Comparison of magnetic tapes

Tape type	*Tape length*	*Capacity (MB)*	*Recording method*	*Density (bpi)*
4 mm DAT	60 m	1.3 (2.6 GB)	Helical scan	1,869 tpi
	90 m	2(4) GB	helical scan	1,69 tpi
8 mm DAT	60 ft	2.3 GB		5,400
	112 m	5(10) GB	helical scan	8,500
TK 25	0.25" X 600 ft	60	10-track	8,000
TK 50	0.5" X 600 ft	60	Serpent, 22-track	6,667
TK 70	0.5" X 600 ft	296	Serpent, 48-track	10,000
QIC-11	600 ft	60	9-track	NA
QIC-24	600 ft	60	9-track	8,000
QIC-120	600 ft	125	15-track	10,000
QIC-150	1000 ft	250	18-track	10,000
QIC-320	600 ft	320	26-track	16,000
QIC-525	1000 ft	525	26-track	16,000
IBM-3480		200	Linear, 18-track	NA
Typical reel	0.5" X 2400 ft	145	Linear, 9-track	6,250

more reliable because the influence of one tape winding on other windings is less due to larger separation of the magnetic coating.

4.1.4. Digital Audio Tape

It is the most common device used for archival storage and retrieval of large volumes of data. Digital recording on magnetic tape was developed for use in sound recording in the 1970s and for the consumer market by the late 1980s. Digital recorders convert audio signals into data on a magnetic tape by means of a microprocessor (analogue-to-digital) and reconvert the data back into analogue audio signals (digital-to-analogue) for playback with the amplifier of a conventional stereo sound system.

Although intended for ordinary domestic use, the system has not been successful with the general public, but it is now widely used for professional purposes, including sound recording for motion pictures. DAT machines have also been adapted for the recording of digital computer data, and to record sound, which would not be picked up using other means.

The medium on which information is recorded, stored and read with the help of laser light, with a view to increase its storage capacity. Hence it is also known as compact medium. They offers very high recording densities then the magnetic media, discussed earlier. As against tapes and disks which utilize magnetic fields to orient magnetic partials in desired direction, optical storage systems user laser to record information by selectively altering the light reflectance characteristics of specially designed media.

Deals with optical media that includes : read-only discs, write-once-read many optical discs and erasable optical discs. Defines the concept of Optical storage and describes the physical character of optical disc and its characteristics in terms of durability, high storage and portability. Read-only optical discs are discussed in details. Highlights the CD-ROM discs, their physical character and manufacturing process. Discusses the manufacturing, mastering processes that include premastering and replication with merits and demerits in detail. Highlights some standards of Compact Disc-interactive (CD-I) and Compact Disc-Read-Only Memory Extended Architecture (CD-ROM XM) used for accommodating multimedia information on a compact disc. Explains the characteristics of WORM discs and erasable optical discs, their manufacturing process and merits and demerits over heard discs.

The current era has acquire the name of 'information era'. The new technologies have accelerated the research and development and lead to 'information explosion'. This in turn has made impact on storage, retrieval and dissemination of information. Due to this exponentional growth of information and information sources, the print media is becoming obsolete and the media for information storage are fast changing in a fascinating manner.

Some of the storage media are :

* Print Media (Paper, metal sheets etc.)
* Film Media (Microfilm, Microfiche etc.)
* Magnetic Media (Magnetic tape, disc, drum etc.)
* Electronic Media (Floppy disc, hard discs etc.)
* Optical Media (CD-ROM, Video disc, CD-WORM, CD-I etc.)

4.2. OPTICAL DISCS

An optical disc is relatively inexpensive and has a life span of about 10-50 years. Its high storage capacity makes it appropriate not only for storing relatively large data but also the full text of the documents and images, graphics and video images as well as sound.

Broadly optical discs can be grouped into 3 categories :

1. Read-Only Optical Discs,
2. Write-Once Read Many Optical Discs,
3. Erasable Optical Discs.

4.2.1. Read-Only Optical Discs

In this type of optical discs, the information or data is recorded by the manufacturers and the end user receives only a read only disc, which is played in a player in order to read the data, audio, video information that has been recorded on the disc. Nothing can be written (added) or removed on this types of discs. There are different kinds of read-only discs that have found wide applications.

4.2.1.1. Video Discs

These discs were developed for the distribution of pre-recorded videos. Hybrid video discs store different types of information on a single disc including text data, and high quality video. One side of the video disc can store or hold about ½ hour movie pictures or programmes. Luck of standards and high cost of hardware has restricted their adaptation.

4.2.1.1.1. Digital Video Interactive (DV-1)

It integrates both audio and video. With DV-1, full motion pictures could be stored on a CD.DV-I is expected to store around one hour worth of motion picture on one disc. DV-1 is being developed as a computer peripheral and electronic products.

4.2.1.1.2. Compact Discs

CDs are very popular consumer products in the market as audio playback. They were designed to store huge amount of data and tom provide high facility of sound using a digital recording technique. Since its introduction, CDs have become popular at an extremely rapid rate and discs are widely available form a number of manufacturers. Some recognized CDs CD-Digital Audio (CDDA), CD-Read-only memory (CD-ROM), CD-ROM extended Architecture (CD-ROM XA), CD-Recordable (CD-R) and CD-Interactive (CD-I).

4.2.1.1.3. CDDA

In CDDA information is coded and stored on the disc in digital form, but at playback stage this gets converted into analog form and the audio signals are played back using amplifiers.

4.2.1.1.4. Compact Disc-Read-Only Memory (CD-ROM)

In recent times, CD-ROM drives have become a part of the standard configuration of a PC, be it for corporate, academic, R & D or home usage. It has become a de facto drive along with the 3.5-inch floppy disc drive.

The growth of multimedia titles, games,

entertainment and cheap availability of videodiscs, and the latest trend in software distribution through CDs made CD-ROM discs and drives more popular. Also, there is a gradual increase in the digital information component in R & D, corporate and academic libraries, which are moving towards handling digital information slowly. New libraries are also joining the stream by slowly introducing CD-ROM databases. It is the first practical technology for mass distribution, which is suited to the developing countries where the communication infrastructure is rather poor. All these factors are making CD-ROM more and more popular for the office as well as home usage.

The CD-ROM, a 12-cm and 1.2-mm thick disc can hold approximately 650-680 million characters (650-680 MB) equal to about 2,70,000 pages of (A4) plain text or about 60,000 suitably compressed images. The advantages of CD-ROM are its huge storage capacity, durability, transportability, light weight, easy and faster (200 ms) access to and non-corruptibility of stored information, immunity to magnetic fields and amenability for parallel searching by multiple users in a Local Area Network (LAN) or Wide Area Network (WAN) environment CD-ROM, the 'digital] papyrus, has become synonymous with electronic publishing. Due to these qualities the publishers of scholarly periodicals, reference books (including encyclopedias, dictionaries, handbooks, cottages, etc.), multimedia products, and bibliographic databases have increasingly used it. Almost all software released in the market is now distributed on CD-ROM.

The popular application and penetration of CD-ROM in the market can be observed from the number of CD-ROM discs, drives and products sold during the last few years. About 1.1 million CD-ROM discs were pressed in January 1992 which by Dec 1992 rose four-fold to 4.4 million. The number of CD-ROMs sold during the last quarter of 1993 was more than the total number sold during the previous three quarters of the year.

The installed base of CD-ROM drives was 2.3 million in 1990 which in 1995 rose to 37 million and was expected to reach 100 million drives by 1998. Due to the use of multimedia products, this increasing further. A majority of PCs sold are bundled with CD-ROM drives. A 63 per cent growth of CD-ROM titles was achieved during 1992 and 1993, and it was expected to grow more than 300% during 1993 and 1995. According to the 1995 edition of the CD-ROM directory of TFOL, there were about 9,500 titles in market in the autumn of 1994, which represent 50% growth over the titles available in the previous year.

In general, full text databases account for 40% sources followed by bibliographic (25%) and reference work (16%) respectively. Tables 6 shows the growth of CD-ROM drives and titles during 1985-1999. The New Media Directory of the Waterlow New Media Information lists 3,269 publishers who are involved in e-publishing using CD-ROM format, and 32,162 titles including DVD-ROMs and DVD-Videos. Language-wise, English accounts for title over 77% (24,850 titles) followed by German and French.

The speed of CD-ROM drives has changed a lot from the time they were introduced in the late 1980s.

The single speed (1X) drive (at a transfer ate of 150 kbps) of 1987 has been replaced by the double-speed (2X) drives in the early 1990s which in turn gave-way to 4X drives in 1994, 6x drives in 1995, and 8X , 10 X and 12X drives in 1996 which were replaced by 24X drives 1997. Now CD drives up to 48X speeds are available in the market. This speed is progressing further.

Table 6. The growth of CD-ROM title and drives in the market

Year	*No. of CD-ROM titles*	*CD-ROM Drives (millions)*
1985	1	NA
1986	42	NA
1987	96	NA
1988	160	NA
1989	397	NA
1990	820	- 2.3
1991	1,561	- 3.6
1992	2,213	5
1993	3,597	11
1994	5,382	20
1995	7,075	37
1996	12,989	60
1997	9,024	82
1998	27,000	100
1999	32,162	Na

The prices of CD-ROM discs and drives are also falling steeply making it within the reach for many home users. Table 4 shows the cost per MB storage of three media. The high cost of hard disc off-sets its highest retrieval speed [4, 5, 6].

4.2.1.1.4.1. Cd-ROM XA

This format of compact discs have both audio and video capacities. It was designed to accommodate multimedia information on a compact disc. This standard format allows CD-I and CD-ROM discs to be used on either type of disc player.

4.2.1.1.4.2. CD-Interactive

CD- Interactive was developed for the interactive applications that run on a stand-alone player. In this audio signals are played back using amplifiers.

4.2.1.1.4.3. CD-ROM Manufacturing process

The manufacturing process of CD-ROM discs consists of three steps :

(i) Pre-mastering process

(ii) Mastering process

(iii) Replication process

4.2.1.1.4.3.1. Pre-Mastering Process

This process involves the input data preparation and application software development to generate the required pre-master CD-tape. With the help of Data Base Management System (DBMS) the data is prepared in a particular format suitable for the retrieval software. For instance, if the data is tabular, then tabular data structure has to be developed with the help of DBMS. In this process, first the data in required format is stored on a magnetic tape, this data is then transferred in to a CD-ROM Master tape that is normally a U-MATIC or EXABYTE-tape. This tape is then fed into a minicomputer which drives the mastering processes.

4.2.1.1.4.3.2. Mastering Process

This process consists of transferring data from CD-tape to a thin reflective surface of the master disc. The disc has a spiral track divided in to a number of sectors. The total length of the spiral track is about 5 km. For recording the data on disc "Constant Linear Velocity" (CVL) method is used in which the linear velocity of the rotating disc remains constant to the read/write head due to which the disc rotates faster when read/write head is on the inner tracks compared with the outer tracks. Resultant large data can be stored on the outer tracks.

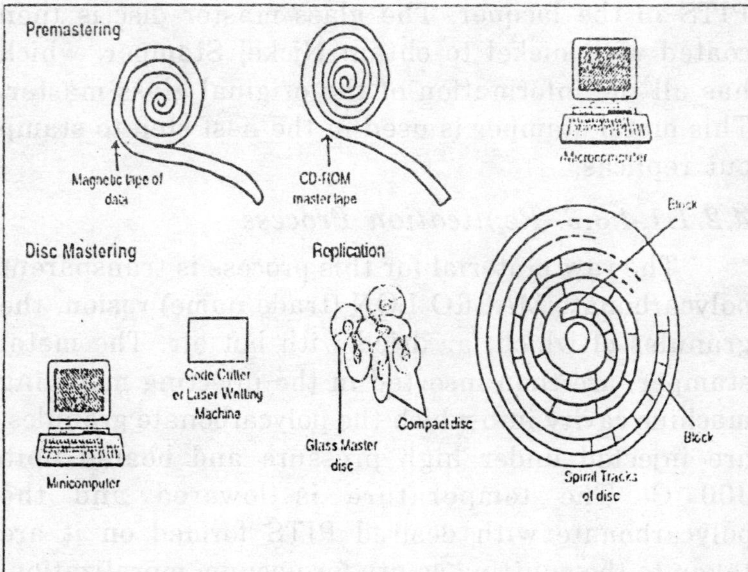

Fig. 10. CD-ROM Manufacturing Process

To encode information on disc, a laser writing machine (code cutter controlled by minicomputer) is used to produce a lacquer coating glass master disc, the density of the laser beam required for recording the date is 25 mw. The laser beam is switched on and off. According to the codified information on the computer tape. On receiving signals, the laser beam aimed at blank rotating master disc vaporized microscopic portion to form tiny holes called PITS. The absence of signals leaves the surface intact. On the disc surface, the data is stored as a series of PITS (data) and LANDS (No data), which corresponds to magnetestised and non-magnetized digital data. The width of a PIT is 0.6 microns and the distance between two tracks is 1.6 macrons. The information is stored on the spiral track of disc consisting od tiny PITS in the lacquer. The glass master disc is then coated with nickel to obtain Nickel Stamper, which has all the information of the original glass master. This metal stamper is used in the nest step to stamp out replicas.

4.2.1.1.4.3.3. Replication Process

The raw material for this process is transparent polycarbonate MACRO LON (trade name) resion, the granules of which, ar dried with hot air. The metal stamper, are then inserted in the injecting moulding machine cavity into which the polycarbonate granules, are injected under high pressure and heated upto 300 C. The temperature is lowered and the polycarbonate with desired PITS formed on it are taken to the sputting cavity for vacuum moralization. The metal vapours provide the reflective AI or Ni coating. To protect the CD from contamination and surface damage, clear lacquer coating is applied by spin coating process. After further clearing, the label printing is done on the back of the disc giving information about the contents.

CD-ROM eventually has become a new too for storage, retrieval and distribution of vast data or information. CD-ROM discs have spiral tracks which are divided into a number of sectors. Each sector or block on CD-ROM discs actually contains some 98 CD-frames, each of 24 bytes to give a total sector capacity of 2352 bytes of which 2048 bytes are always for user data and reaming 304 bytes are used for the codification purpose. The codes are appended to the front and back of the user data. These codes consist of header, synchronization , error detection and error correction bytes and the bytes that drives need to locate data on disc illustrated bellow :

Table 7. CD-ROM Discs spiral tracks

Synchronization field	12 Bytes
Header field	04 Bytes
User data	2048 Bytes
Auxiliary data	288 Bytes
Total	**2352**

4.2.1.1.4.4. To read the Data

For reading data from the disc, a lower density (5mw) laser beam is used. The data is stored on the surface as a series of PITS and LANDS of variable length. A PIT is a small dent (0.6 micron) and LAND is the surface between PITS. In operation, when laser beam of lower density focuses on the rotating surface, the PITS scatter the laser beam and the LANDS reflect it. The direction and amount of reflect light changes as the surface changes from LANDS to PITS and vice versa. These changes in the light are detected by the reading head and give CD-drive to read data. The CD-ROM reading head does not get close to the disc as in the case of magnetic read/write head. Hence the chance of the head crashing into disc is virtually zero.

4.2:1.1.4.5. Comparison With Magnetic Disc

The comparison of a CD-ROM disc with a heard disc is given below :

Table 8. Comparison of CD-ROM Disc and Hard Disc

	CD-ROM	*Hard Disc*
Capacity	600 MB	10-40 MB
Number of tracks	18,000	612
Average seek	500	100
Rotational Speed	300-600 rpm	3600 rpm
Average latency	100 ms	8.3 ms
Transfer rate	150 mb/sec	96 kb/sec

4.2.1.1.4.6. Library Applications of CD-ROM

The contents of CD-ROM products generally include abstracts, databases, full-length articles, images, audio and software. CD-ROM databases are cost-affective. CD-ROMs have many library-specific applications. CD-ROM offers a number of advantages as well as avenues for applications and not surprisingly, libraries are major customers of CD-ROM products.

The enormous data capacity of CD-ROM makes it ideal for a wide range of applications from publishing to :

(a) Facilitate collection development, evaluation, print purchase orders, procedure card catalogue and quantitative/citation studies as databases like Books-in-Prints Plus with about 2 million records and a number of indexes offer such flexibility;

(b) Serve as reference tools;

(c) Support current awareness service (CAS) and selective dissemination of information (SDI) as it possible to provide contents, abstracts, full text etc and also facilitate information retrieval by a specific journal name;

(d) Allow expanded quality of services, enhanced number of users, exhaustive coverage of information at little or no extra cost or time;

(e) Are viable and cost-effective alternative to online searching though not as current as online databases;

(f) Facilitate library automation, retro-conversion of bibliographic data as well as cataloguing since many OPACs of individual or groups of libraries are available on CD-ROMs;

(g) Are amenable for retrospective searching as back files are also available in many cases;

(h) Facilitate networking, library cooperation, searching by multi and remotely-located users, and resource sharing;

(i) Help in saving of resources as less-used journals can be discontinued if they are included in bibliographic databases and only those articles needed form such journals can be procured based on CAS and SDI services;

(j) Involve lesser transit delays and provide more current information than print media;

(k) Enhance the image of the library and serve as excellent public relation tools, especially in the present environment of marketing of information products;

(l) Allow exchange of bibliographic data, software, etc.; and

(m) Are ideal for archival purpose of gray literature like internal reports, newspapers, reports, standards, and patents.

4.2.1.1.4.6. Advantages of CD-ROM Discs

CD-ROM Discs have a lot of advantages. There are :

(a) **High Storage Capacity** : CD-ROM discs have tremendous storage capacity as compared magnetic storage media.

(b) **Multimedia Capacity** : CD-ROM discs have multimedia capacity as different types of data viz. conventional text and numeric data with audio, computer graphics, video or digital photographic images can coexist on a single CD-ROM disc. These data can be accessed simultaneously which is not possible with other storage media.

(c) **Enhanced Retrieval Capacities** : It offers powerful method of information retrieval such as free text, controlled vocabulary searching and combining of concepts through Boolean logic. Some CDs provide menu-driven for the experienced searchers.

(d) **Easy and Unlimited Access** : CD-ROM products

provide an easy and unlimited access to the stored information as and when needed. The disc can be used repeatedly and allow unlimited access to the information similar to books.

(e) **PCs and CD-ROM** : CD-ROM is a powerful peripheral for personal computers and with the use of CD-drives, PCs can be transformed into a very powerful information resources. A convenient way of database searching can be obtained by combining PCs and CD-ROMs.

(f) **Controlled Cost** : The cost of manufacturing discs and their distribution is low as compared to the amount of data it stores. The expensive access to large mainframe systems can be diminished by using CD-ROM data base on PCs. the costs of CD-ROMs are independent of the amount of searching time.

(g) **Portability and Durability** : CD-ROMs being small in size, are easily portable and have high durability i.e. their storage life is about 10-50 years.

(h) **Psychological Advantage** : Searching on CD-ROM has a definite psychological advantage because the users are free from time pressure, they can try various strategies to obtain optimum results and there is no financial penalty for committing mistakes.

(i) **Data Protection** : On CD-ROMs it is possible to maintain the integrity, purity and performance of data since there is no chance of accidental data erasure, head crash and any wear and tear because the R/W head does not touch the surface of the disc.

(j) **Easy Storage** : Like floppy it can be removed from the drive giving it mobility.

4.2.1.1.4.8. Disadvantages of CD-ROMs

Besides a lot of disadvantages is long access time as compared to hard discs and online searching. Response rate is also very slow. Only one user can access a CD-ROM at one time so other have to wait for their turn.

(a) **Read-Only device** : Since it is a read-only device, the currency of information can not be maintained.

(b) **Lack of Standardization** : It is a major barrier of CD-ROM. Standardization is essential for the flexibility. Through standardization, hardware and software incapabilities and differences in operating procedures can be minimized.

4.2.1.1.5. Digital Video Disc (DVD)

Digital video disc, or Digital Versatile Disc the computer industry, is the next generation to Compact Disc in optical disc storage technology. A DVD looks just like a Cd (both 120 mm diameter), but has higher data storage capacity. Like a CD, data is recorded on DVD in a spiral trail on tiny pits, and the discs are read using a laser beam.

The DVD's larger capacity is achieved by making the pits smaller and the spiral tighter, and by recording the data in as many as four layers, two on each side of the disc. To read these tightly packed discs, lasers that produce a shorter wavelength beam of light are required, as are more accurate aiming and focusing mechanisms.

The main feature of DVD is the compression technology and storage data on multi-layer sides. A single sided-single layer DVD holds 4.7 GB and two-layer DVD can hold 8.5 GB of data. There are other DVD formats with double-sided specifications. A double sided-single layer DVD can hold about 9.5 GB and double-sided double layer DVD can hold about 17 GB of data.

4.2.1.1.5.1. Types of DVD

There are various kinds of DVD's :

(i) DVD-ROM;
(ii) DVD-Audio;
(iii) DVD-Video;
(iv) DVD-Recordable;
(v) DVD-Erasable

2.1.1.5.2. Comparison of DVD and CD Charecteristics

Table 9. Comparison of CD-ROM and DVD

	DVD	***CD***
Diameter	120 mm	120 mm
Thickness	0.663 mm	1.2 mm
1.6 nanometers	0.764 nanometers	1.6 nanometers
Min Pit Length	0.46 nanometers	0.834 nanometers
Laser Wavelength	640 nm	780 nm
Data capacity (Per Layer)	4.7 GB	0.68 GB
Layers	1, 2, 3	1

2.1.1.5.3.Advantages of DVD Multimedia Reference Sources on DC Sources

* The high data storage capacity of DVDs makes

it possible to represent more multimedia elements, like sound and video and many integrate many reference sources on a single disc.

* The quality of sound and video in DVD is better than CD-ROM. In fact, DVD makes it possible to display longer full screen, full motion and high quality videos.
* DVD can deliver the data at a higher rate than CD-ROM.
* DVD drives can read both CD-ROMs and DVD-ROM's.
* By using DVD databases it might be possible to avoid CD-ROM jukeboxes.
* DVD eliminates the need for disc swapping of deluxe multimedia databases and makes information-seeking information more convenient.
* No telecommunication facility is essential as in the case of Web.
* Printing and downloading the information is feasible.
* Multi-lingual databases can be handled.
* Better security of data.

2.1.1.5.4. Library Applications

The most important and relevant applications of this new technology in libraries may include the following areas

* Large full text databases.
* Mixed databases.
* Quick reference databases.
* Very high quality multimedia will help in better reference service.

* Archival Purposes.
* Cost-effective mass storage for networking purposes.
* Preservation media for multimedia libraries etc.
* Training applications.

Textual and multimedia reference source on CD-ROM revolutionized library reference services. Now we have the novel, advanced technology of DVD to store gigabytes of bibliographic, full-text and multimedia databases.

4.2.2.Write Once-Read Many Media (WORM)

When introduced in the early 1980s, no standard format was available and WORM optional discs appeared in 5.25; 8-, 12- and 14-inch sizes. However, in the 1990s the 5.25- and 12-inch discs and drives started stabilizing. The data storage capacities depend upon the number of recording surface, which can vary from one to four. A 5.25-inch disc can hold 400 MB to 1.2 GB whereas its 12-inch counterpart can hold from 2 to 6.6 GB of data, using jukebox technology, this could be increased further for archival storage of enormous volumes of data CR-R and DVD-R are the two important WORM technologies having potential application in libraries.

Initially the WORM optional discs were not meant for publishing applications; rather these were introduced for use in digital audio and video market. Later, after realizing their potential, these were adapted for low cost, high capacity, computer storage peripherals. In a WORM disc, data can be recorded only once, but can be retrieved any number of times.

The recorded data is immune to erasure and rewriting if not possible. So WORM discs are ideally suited for archival applications in libraries, banking and insurance sectors.

4.2.2.1. CD-Recordable

The major problems in the production CD-ROM were the high data preparation and mastering costs. However, it has low cost of replication. The prices of CD-ROM have been falling steeply since its introduction in the market. The introduction of CD-R (or WORM) in the market in recent times, makes the medium much cheaper. While the earliest WORM discs were of 100 or 200 MB capacity, the latest ones (CD-R) can store up to 600 MB of data. Standardized in 1989, CD-R become a tremendous success with corporate and professional set-ups. Its is fast catching up with CD-ROM in popular acceptance and usage. It has been estimated that there were 2 million units of CD-R hardware in 1995 which was expected to reach 27 million by 1998. If the market trend is any indication, the gap between the two would be lesser than the predicted one. Just as the blank audio and video cassettes and floppy discs outsell the pre-recorded ones, CD-Rs too are expected to outsell CD-ROMs in a few years.

The cheap availability of CD-R drives which were too expensive till recently, makes it easy to create a CD-ROM of one's own database for a paltry sum JVC's Personal RoomMaker, HP Sure Store CD-Writer 4020i, Olympus Delties CD-R2/ISA, Optima Discovery 650 CR-R, Sony Spressa 920 and Philip's CDD 522 Compact Disc Recorder are a few recording devices. Each of these includes suitable software bundled with them which allows users to pre-master and master their own CD-ROMs in-house. These are available on both PC and Mac versions.

Starting 1996, the prices of CD-R hardware as well as blank discs have been slashed. This has, no doubt, encouraged in-house production system. This is economical and versatile as producing one's own CD takes only about 45 minutes to an hour. At present 8X (i.e. 1200 kbps) speed is common. This may further improve when the recording speeds increase and when the CD-R hardware is customized to include build-in hard drives or tape drives to make recording more convenient.

CD-R is found to be useful for in-house publishing of a large data files, creating multimedia products, downloading and distribution of shareware, it is an ideal archiving medium for in-house databases, as the user can simply download the data from the computer system on the recordable disc. CD-R is also a medium for capturing, storage and retrieval of coded data, text, scanned images and even voice. However, it is not a primary publishing medium.

4.2.2.2. DVD-R

DVD-ROM is a read-only format and does not allow the creation of back up of huge data files or distribution discs of software, etc. To fill this gap DVD-R and DVD-RAM have been introduced in the market in 1998. DVD-R discs, analogous to CD-R, allow information to be written once and read subsequently any number of times.

4.2.3. Erasable/Rewritable Media

The erasable optical media is regarded as the

third generation optical storage device technology. There are two types of otional discs, viz., CD-Rewritable) CD-RW, also known as CD-Erasable or CD-E) and DVD-RAM/DVD+RW, which are amenable for writing, erasing and rewriting data any number of times.

4.2.3.1. CD-RW

Although introduced in 1988, CD-RW technology was made available in 1996 and met with tremendous success. CD-RW discs differ with WORM discs in that these allow erasing and rewriting over stored data. In the 5.25-inch size, they resemble magnetic discs and provide random access. However they are slower with about 650 kbps data transfer rate and access time of 70-120 ms. These discs like magnetic media, are amenable to store, read, record, erase and re-record data on the same area of the disc any number of times, This property makes it a potential contender for computer peripheral applications, where the files are regularly retrieved and re-recorded. This technology is expected to complete with magnetic disc storage as it offers higher storage capacity, low-cost drives, durability, unlimited off-line storage and automatic disc handling through jukebox. Due to falling prices, the CD-RW drives have become affordable making them ideal alternative mass storage devices. This trend would continue as the multi-read specifications make.

CD-RW media read-compatible with CD-R and in future with CD-ROM and drives. Although the market for CD-ROM is still growing, it is expected that, by the end of year 2000, the recordable and rewritable optical storage will represent up to 40% of the total optical disc drive market. A CD-RW can hold about 2.5 GB per side, i.e., 5 GB per disc. By the year of 2000, a DSDL CD-RW disc may be available which can hold 10 GB of data. While CD-R discs are cheap, CD-RW discs are costly Table 6 shows the current and projected sales of CD-RW drives.

Table 10. Sales of CD-RW and DVD+RW drives during 1998-2002.

Year	*Number of units sold (millions)*	
	CD-RW	***DVD+RW***
1998	4.1	0.112
1999	10.5	0.545
2000	17.3	1.5
2002	22.3	7.3

4.2.3.2. DVD-RAM and DVD+RW

The DVD-RAM disc permits and unlimited number of writings on to and reading from the disc, and is analogues to the CD-RW format. Whereas DVD-R discs can hold 3.9 GB of data, the capacity of DVD-RAM hold 2.6 GB. DVD+RW, a variant of DVD-RAM, is also a read/rewrite disc with a capacity of 3 GB. The main difference between the two formats is that the DVD-RAM requires a special cartage to hold the disc since handling can spoil the sensitive surface of the disc, this cartage is not required by DVD+RW (24). This is the result of two different groups of developers with compositions of different companies that are behind DVD-RAM and the DVD+RW formats. In the DVD-RAMs data are recorded both within the grooves and on the lands between grooves. Also, both have different ways for recording physical address information that ultimately results in the increased capacity of DVD+RW format.

DVD+RW is compatible with most of DVD players whereas the DVD-RAM is not. This is reflected in the acceptance and sales (Table 10) of DVD+RW. DVD-RAM drives can copy 315 MB of data in about 12 minutes. These are flexible for reading and writing DVD-RAM discs (up to 5.2 GB). These drives can also read CD-ROM, CD-R, CD-RW and DVD-ROM discs.

4.2.3.3. Optional discs and Electronic Publishing

Optional discs have become synonymous with electronic publishing (e-publishing). CD-ROMs, videodiscs and online bibliographic databases form a major part of the e-publishing field. CD-ROMs have penetrated all branches of professional and scholarly publishing. This is because of success of the CD-ROM as the optical medium of choice for the publishing industry and also due to its acceptance by major libraries around the world. Durability, capability to hold large volumes of data, and affordability are the important factors for the success of CD-ROMs. Many publishers including McGraw-Hill, Wiley, Elsevier, North-Holand, Meckler, Grolier, Prentice-Hall, Oxford University, etc. have all ventured in this area. CD-ROMs are slowly inching towards replacing microform documents primarily due to their versatility, low cost and ease of use. The usability of CD-ROMs in a networking environment made this technology more attractive and acceptable to the library community.

Electronic publishing replaced the printed reference source to a large extent, secondary and some tertiary periodicals followed suit. The primary journals embraced CD-ROM rather slowly. Many publishes like Elsevier, ADONIS, IEEE, Chemical Abstract Service, Cambridge Science Abstracts, SCI, BIOSIS, INSPEC, etc.

In recent times CD-ROM publishing systems have been on the rise. Besides creating searchable versions of database and storing them on CD-ROM, these allow anyone to become a CD-ROM publisher/ producer. These systems facilitate libraries and other institutions that are involved in creating databases of their holdings (and archives) to produce CD-ROM-based searchable products and to market them.

The latest development in e-publishing is the Web publishing. The World Wide Web is offering limitless opportunities for becoming one's own publisher. The Web provides seamless access to the (published) information, without any restriction. Many document publishing systems enable Internet publishing and even support the indexing of unstructured documents while providing full text searching capabilities for users. Internet document publishing process, features of document publishing systems including list of a few such systems and document publishing of the Web have been dealt in detail elsewhere. The advent of Web publishing has facilitates the speed of publishing. Although initially these were distributed in ASCII text files through listservs, the Web browsers like Mosaic and Gopher or FTP protocols later started providing access to e-journals on the Net. Current technology provides hypertext links which connect references to other articles/journals and other Web files.

4.2.3.4. Hybrids

The choice of publication medium changes as per the situational need and depends upon various considerations including cost, availability of equipment, frequency of up-dation, and other factors. in situation where text, graphics and video (including animation) are part of a publication, CD-ROM emerged as the best medium for e-publishing. Networks, Intranets and Internet became the publishing media when the environment warranted continuous updation. In such an hybrid environment, CD-ROMs combined with online networks have become popular and acceptable hybrid publication media.

The CD-ROM/online hybrids allow the user searching a database or an encyclopedia on CD-ROM to get connected through internet to forums, e-publications, news services and chat rooms relevant to the subject. Thus Grolier Electronic Encyclopedia includes more than 12,000 links through Compu Serve (America Online, AOL). World Book Encyclopedia (1998) of IBM links to a site offering current news and updates to the CD.

Many major encyclopedias of 1998 offer online connections. Database vendors like Knight-Ridder On-Disc (Dialog), and LEXIS-NEXIS allow users access updated information on their files being searched; these also allow users of the respective CD-ROMs save search strategies and then log on to the online files to search and download results. A number of CD-ROM periodicals (for example, Media Magazine) with online links have been introduced.

Some have links to Internet. AOL also offers Compton's interactive Encyclopedia, and 2 Market-a hybrid CD-ROM shopping service; Time Almanac, multimedia game sand buyers guides. The Multimedia and CD-ROM Directory of TFPK Multimedia listed 600 hybrid title in mid-1997, an increase of 160 per cent from January 1997. It is likely that the same trend will be observed in future too. Also many CD-ROM publishers are offering their publications on Internet.

4.2.3.5. Volume Holographic Storage Technology

Holographic storage technique facilitates 3-D storage of data as against the 2-D storage achieved by magnetic or optical routes. In holographic memory, information is stored as a pattern generated by two mutually coherent beams split from the same laser source. A plane wave serves as the reference beam. When the two beams intersect in a photosensitive material, they form an interference, or fringe pattern which is trapped by the material. At the time of retrieval, when the recorded fringe pattern, which is illuminated by the original reference beam, the spatially modulated pattern is produced through optical diffraction. In volume holography, by exploiting the Brag effect, multiple interference fringe pattern are superimposed in the same volume and reconstructed without cross talk. To pack several fringe patterns into one location, each is recorded using a reference beam with a Brag angle unique to the pattern. This is achieved by employing may of the three techniques in use.

In the first, a rotating mirror is employed to deflect reference beam to different angles. The second technique uses a 2-D array of surface-emitting semiconductor lasers to generate angularly distinct beams. A third technique employs lenses to convert the spatial position of a beam source into angle. Photo-polymers and 'photo-refractive class of materials are used as volume holographic materials. A 30 X 30 mm holographic card can hold 1 GB data. Future developments in the laser array, spatial light modulator, and volume holographic material technologies would greatly facilitate the success of volume holographic storage as an acceptable mass storage technology.

4.3. OPTICAL CHARACTER RECOGNITION (OCR)

Optical Character Recognition (OCR) uses reflected light to identify the individual characters contained in documents thus it converts printed characters into electronic signals that can be processed by computers. In other words the process of reading characters of a source document by an optical character reader is known as optical character recognition.

According to Aptagiri, ORC has two essential steps, namely.

1. Scanning,
2. Recognition.

Rao Kamath on the other hand have mentioned one move step namely documents transport which can be explained as follows.

4.3.1. Document Transport

Document Transport denote the movement of each document to the reading station, position the document properly, and move the some into an output hopper. The transport mechanism following are the two types.

1. For handling individual documents
2. For handling continuous rolls

4.3.2. Scanning

Optical scanning device is used scan a page and store the resultant image in a computer. Textual data is scanned using a scanner. Optical scanner is a device which can tell whether a maker is present on a piece of paper by measuring the amount of light reflected from the paper Optical scanning devices are variously described as, document scanner, page scanners, document digitizers, or image digitizes'.

Scanning

↓

Matrix Matching Method | Feature Extraction Method

4.3.2.1. Matrix Maching Device

Matrix Matching denotes a sort of comparison of a character against the stored matrix of the same character, and their by, recognizes it.

4.3.2.2. Feature Extraction Method

Feature extension method, the broad features of each characters are store and the characters are compared against this, using either enlarging or ordering techniques if necessary.

4.3.3. Recognition

The main task of the recognition system is to translate the stored image into textual information.

The OCR system converts the analog signal pattern form each pixed and digitized it into to matrix of binary data.

4.3.3.1. Mark-Sense Recognition

Mark-sensing refers to the reading of specialized pencil mark on documents are question papers are things alike by means of an optical mark reader.

4.3.3.2. Barcode Label Recognition

In bar code label recognition, a specially designed label consisting of closely spaced lines of varying widths is use to encode a numeric identifier. A typical barcode label measures 1.5. to 2 inch wide by 0.6 to 0.75 inches high. In edition to the barcode it self, the label may contain the barcode numbering human readable form and other printed information. Some of the popular example barcode patterns are :

1. Code 3 to 9 (Described as code 39)
2. Code bar, and
3. Interleaved 2 to 5.

Most of the barcode formats employ a 14 to 16 digit number. Code labels which may be affixed to documents or other or objects are read by specially designed scanners that interpret the numbers they represent and designed scanners that interpret the numbers they represent and transmit them to a computer. Barcode scanner is an optical device used to decode the information present on any document or object.

4.3.4. Optical Reading /Sensing

An optical mark reader reads the recordings of marks on documents and the data is often written to magnetic tape ready for processing. A variety of optical readers are available to address myriad applications.

4.3.4.1. Optical Mark Reader

An optical mark reader senses the minute black spot created by special pencil on form and restores the data a magnetic tape, disc or punched cards comparing the same with standard data. Optical mark readers are commonly used to read the answers on computer test papers.

4.3.4.2. Optical Page Reader

Optical page reader senses the input device optically that accepts a page of printed matter.

4.3.4.3. Optical Character Reader

It is an optically sensing device that accepts a printed document as input reads them by identifying characters according to their shapes.

4.3.4.4. Optical Senser Reader

It is a first type of reader with a speed of 100 cards per minute or 1000 characters per second. It utilizes a light source and Ploto cells. As the tape passes through the pattern of light passing shining through the holes is converted by the photo cells into a pattern of electronic pulses.

4.3.5. Optical Printer

Printer is an important output peripheral irrespective of the system application, some of the printers that use optical technology are as under.

4.3.5.1. Electrostatic/Optical Printer

Optical printers are also termed as Electrostatic

printers. It is a nonimpact printer that prints Dot matrix characters one at a time by means of wires or pins that supply an electrical changes in the desired patterns on to an aluminum coated particles of dry ink adhere to the magnetized areas and are then fixed by heat.

4.3.5.2. Laser Printer

Laser printer is also a non-impact printer that uses laser beam to create dot matrix characters on a photo conductor which are then transferred to paper one page at a time. Laser printers are preferred for applications requiring high quality and varied typographic capabilities. They print on to single sheets of letter size bound paper rather than the fan-folded stock used by chain printers and dot matrix printers Laser printer can intermix typefaces, sizes and styles with in a single page.

4.3.5.3. Optical font

Optical font denotes a printing font or style of character specially designed to accurately read by reading machines and by people. The most widely used font is OCR-A and OCR-B, which is well defined in internationally, recognized standards.

4.3.6. Optical Fiber

It is an important transmission medium in optical technology. Optical fiber is an electrical transmission cable made up of head of highly sophisticated and transparent glass. The use of the optical fibers is rapidly becoming standard in computer communications.

4.3.6.1. Impact of Web and Online

The recent spread of Internet connectivity in

the world has led to a belief that online is the sustainable alternative to disc storage technology. It is certainly true that the Internet allows access to many more remote information source s than a limited number CD/DVD-ROM's. There is an unmistakable migration from CD/DVD-ROM based products towards Web-based information resources accessed via the Internet. Web is the one user interface and the ideal environment for providing access to remote and frequently updated resources. Despite the diminishment of CD-ROM and DVD in the multiuser arena, there is no reason to believe that these technologies will die out in the near future, but Web will be the favorite medium for libraries. Now people started to speak about bandwidth instead of gigabytes and other technical terms related to storage media.

4.4. FUTURE TRENDS

The latest trend in optical media is towards High Density CD (HDCD), DVD, and introducing a 24 GB disc. There drives when fit into jukeboxes, for greater automated access of data, may provide thousands of GB. Hybrid jukeboxes which can accept CDs, optical discs, or digital linear tapes to provide storage capacities of the order of a few Terabytes (TB) are being developed. While CD-R brought the pre-mastering and mastering to the desktop, efforts are underway to develop variant products of CD and DVD with enhanced or new features. The DVD family is expected to replace CD-ROM and its variants.

An erasable or rewritable medium has potential multimedia applications. The digital technology is diminishing the gap between entertainment and information, and education and recreation. With enhanced data transfer rates and a few GB online capacity, DVD is being seen as a replacement to VCR. By the turn of the century, the market of CD-ROM is expected to be surpassed by DVD drives which is likely to touch 80 millions. DVD drives include an add-in card to handle MPEG-2 (Motion Picture Expert Group-2) video and this will make it popular for home viewers in the years to come. A DVD recorder may be used to record programmes digitally instead of on videotapes.

However, it should be pointed out that the multiplicity of players always led to disagreement in standards resulting in customer confusion. Except for the 800 to 1,600 bpi magnetic tape, which withstood the test of time, others have been fraught with disagreement and incompatibility, amongst their developers. Optical storage, unlike the magnetic media which was regarded as long-term archival standard, is used both for online and archival applications. This board range coupled with competition for market share, resulted in a variety of form factors, speeds, media formats, capacities and the resulting disagreement on standards. Until an agreement on a common standard for the various factors is evolved, these pose problems to the end-users.

One more problem raised by the technology concerns with the shelf life. Many optical media claim a shelf life of 100 years and more. Since no single standards is available for long-term storage, the technology obsolescence factor is to be taken into consideration. The rate of technological advances coupled with merges, sell outs, and closures over the last few years in these areas makes one to wonder if any of these vendors will be there to support their technology even a few decades from now. It is also difficult to except that the current technology does not change further and will be viable for a long period of time.

They magneto-optic technology is expected to play a vital role in mass storage applications in the near future. Also, volume holographic storage, which is 3-D storage as against the present 2-D storage, may be a strong contender for mass storage. The scene may move from MBs and GBs to TBs and PBs (petabytes). Electronic trap technology and proximal prove techniques using stomic force microscope or scanning tunneling microscope are being pursued towards finding an ideal mass storage media for the future.

4.4.1. FMD-ROM

The latest in the storage technology area is the development of the Fluorescent Multi-layers (FM) technology. It enable to store 140 GB on a single disc of regular-sized FMD-ROM technology that is based on a 2-D optical memory, the FMD technology is based on 3-D fluorescence of chemicals in the pits and grooves. When stimulated by a laser beam, the florescent chemicals produce coherent and incoherent light. Data is stored only in incoherent light, which allows multi-layering making the device to have multi layers of stored data that can be read simultaneously. The technology is expected to be available in about a year when FMD-ROM, irregular sized 10-layer disc of 140 GB and a 30-cm 10-layer disc of 140 GB and a 30-cm 10-layer FMD-WORM will be launched in the market.

Archival storage has been a major problem for libraries an librarians. As the stock of a library grows year by year, several problems arise. Major problems associated with conventional print media include the need for a large shelf space, longer retrieval times, expensive maintenance, durability, and wear and tear. These problems made some of the libraries, especially those situated in large cities where addition of extra space is difficult and large libraries with huge collections to resort to either weeding out at regular intervals documents which are not active or create dormitory collection to store unused and less used documents. These factor coupled with the ever-changing technological advances in the electronics and computer technology paved the way for the development of mass storage systems.

REFERENCES

1. Nair, R. Raman., Computer application to library and information services, New Delhi, Ess Ess, 1992. PP 32-60.
2. Ram, R., computer fundamentals: Architecture and organization, New Delhi : Wiley Eastern, 1994. PP 296-297.
3. Meera., Optical Storage Media : CD-ROM. *Annals of Library Science and Documentation*, Vol 45(3), 1998. PP 77-83.
4. Ram, R. **Op cit.** PP 296-97.
5. Roth, J.P., Essential guide to CD-ROM, London : Merkler, 1985, pp 1-35.
6. Mujoo, Munish. Usha., Visualizing an electronic library. **In** : Venugopal, M.V. eds., *Vistas in library, information systems and networks*, Agra : Y.K. 1999. PP 88-94.
7. Meera., **Op cit.** PP 296-326.

8. Walia, P.K., Applications of CD-ROM in libraries. **In:** Chopra, H.R. and Others. Eds. *Library Science and its facts*, Vol. II, New Delhi : Ess Ess, 1998. PP 48-54.

9. Moorthy, A.L. and Karisiddappa, C.R., Mass storage technologies for libraries and information centers. *DESIDOC Bulletin of Information Technology*. Vol 20(5) Sept 2000. PP 3-20.

10. Ramaiah, L.S., Images and Perceptions in library and information science, New Delhi : Ess Ess, 1998. PP 168-174.

11. Husain, Nargis., CD-ROM : An appropriate technology for developing countries. Herald of Library Science, Vol. 29 (1-2), 1988. PP 3-6.

12. Satyanarayana, V.V.V., Compact Disk Technology and NCTIC CD-ROM. **In :** Venugopal, M.V., eds., *Vistas in library information systems and networks*, Agra : Y.K., 1999. PP 88-94.

13. Vijaya, Kumar, J.K.: CD-ROM to DVD-ROM : A new era in electronic publishing of databases and multimedia reference source. *IASLIC Bulletin*, 45(2), 2000. PP 42-54.

14. Kasyappa, M.M. Database system : Design and development, New Delhi : Sterling, 1993. PP 47-48.

15. Panda, K.C. and Karissiddappa, C.R: eds., New dimensions in information science and technology, New Delhi: Parmal, 1993. PP 90-91.

17. Husain, Nargis., **Op cit.**, PP 2-10.

18. Aptagiri, Devika, V., Optical Character Recognition of salvation for the data entry bottleneck. *Library Science with a slant to Documentation and Information Studies*, 32(1), 1995. PP 25-29.

19. Panda, K.C. and Gautam, J.N., In'fo Technology in the cross road: From Ab'acus to Internet, Agra : Y.K. 1999. PP 254-265.

20. Mujoo, Munidshi, Usha., Op cit. PP 87-94.

21. Moorthy and Karisiddappa, C.R., **Op cit.**, 3-20.

5

Hypertext and Hypermedia

Information storage, retrieval and dissemination are a dynamic process. A number of technologies like radio, motion picture, telecommunications, computers, optical storage technology, etc. have added strength in terms of sophistication, speed and accuracy. But, to retrieve the information quickly, especially when the size of information is large, is rather difficult and time consuming. So far there is no foolproof system to store all the information of human knowledge, and retrieve the same as and when required.

A record, if it is to be useful to science, must be continuously extended, it must be stored; and above all it must be consulted. At present only 10% of the information published is in electronic form and the rest is in printed form. It is a big problem to access the 90% of non-electronic information which mainly comes form magazines, newspapers, R & D resorts, reference manuals, personal communications. etc. Above all, information doubles every few years. To store all the literature published in the world and make it easily accessible to users is a gigantic task.

This problem has drawn the attention of pioneers in information field since the second world war.

Hypertext is, before anything else, a visual form. Hypertext embodies information and communications, artistic and effective constructs, and conceptual abstractions a like into symbolic structures made visible on a computer-controlled display. These symbolic structures can then be combined and manipulated by anyone having access to them.

Hypertext structures are often represented as nodes and links where the nodes "contain" text, graphical information, sounds and so on connected by the links, which however may themselves also contain information or at least be labelled. Depending on the interface metaphor the way the program visually depicts its information the distinction between nodes and links is not always represented in hypertext programs; and the contents of the nodes themselves can often function as links.

The text node-including the illustration-contains hidden links to further information about Walt Whitman which the reader can access either by pressing special keys to display them as they are here. Readers can also follow other explicit links in the "map" window of other nodes and links, or by using search commands to find other nodes or links, certain topics, or words and phrases.

In the text window at the right hidden "wireframe" links have been highlighted by the reader, indicating that further information is available about certain words and the illustration of Whitman (note the two white wireframes in the graphic). The map window offers other nodes and links which the reader can access and locates the relationship of the current space to the hypertext. (Whitman Storyspace by Martha Petry and her students at Jackson Community College used by permission.).

Borrowing from the conventions of print culture, those who view, combine, or manipulate hypertexts are commonly referred to as readers while those who create, gather and arrange hypertexts are called writers. Yet hypertext challenges and, many say, obviates these distinctions. Hypertext readers not only choose the order of what they read but in doing so also alter its form by their choices. Also most hypertext systems allow "readers" to add their own material or links to hypertexts. They thus determine its content for themselves, and often for successive readers, and in a very real sense write (or rewrite) hypertexts.

This dissolving of distinctions between writer and reader makes hypertext a valuable tool for learning and information management as well as a revolutionary artistic medium. Indeed some theorists argue that hypertext represents a shift in human consciousness comparable to the shift from orality to print.

Hypertext takes advantage of the computer's ability to retrieve information in any order (random access) and to store it in any form (a hypermedia database). Hypertext enables interaction between viewers of its material and those who created or gathered the material. While such interaction has heretofore largely taken place in successive times and at a distance (asynchronously); simultaneous and multiple (synchronous) systems are already in use in university and industry research settings.

Readers access the symbolic structures of a hypertext electronically in an order which they choose. They may select among possibilities already visually represented for them by successive authors of the hypertext or its previous readers; or they may create new choices by discovering them within, or adding them to, the visual organization of the hypertext. Computer scientist H. Van Dyke Parunak (1991) sees these choices as a variety of Artificial Intelligence where human supply inferences, connections, and natural language processing which computers cannot yet provide.

In any case, readers' choices constitute the current state of the hypertext and, in effect, its form. Since even the simplest hypertexts present an enormous number of reading choices, and since the order of presentation always changes with readers' choices, hypertexts can never be adequately represented in print.

5.1 HYPERTEXT CONTENT HYPERMEDIA, MULTIMEDIA

Thus far the primary visual symbolic structure of hypertext is language printed to the screen but, as hypertext theorist Don Byrd suggests, print is a "content, not the form, of electronic media." When hypertext content extends to digitized sound, animation, video, virtual reality, computer networks, databases, etc., it is referred to us hypermedia.

Hypermedia is electronically rendered in computers and smaller microcomputer-based consumer devices for storing and delivering information and entertainment. These range from "electronic books" and CD-ROM (Compact Disk-Read Only Memory) or CDI (Compact Disk Interactive) devices to "personal assistants," wireless pocket computers connected with telephone and data networks.

"Multimedia" is often (confusingly) adopted as a marketing and technical term by computer manufacturers, software developers, publishers, and other to describe both hypermedia content and the hardware or software which embodies it.

5.2. A HISTORY OF DEFINITIONS OF HYPERTEXT

Like so much of computer science and engineering, hypertext development has been driven by often competing theories of mind. Born of the liberal progressivist agenda of the post-World War II scientific research effort, the development of hypertext has been shaped as much by thinking in cognitive science, literary theory, pedagogy, utopian social thought, and the written and visual arts, as it has been by computer science research into human-computer interfaces, knowledge structures, artificial intelligence, database management and information retrieval.

The convergence of such fields in hyper textual development signals not only a momentous cultural shift from print to new electronic media ("this late age of print," as Jay Bolter terms our time) but also and more importantly, a corresponding shift in the way human think. At each stage of the developing consensus about these shifts, new and sometimes contradictory definitions of hypertext have been advanced. Even so a remarkably consistent line of thinking holds that hypertext in some sense represents

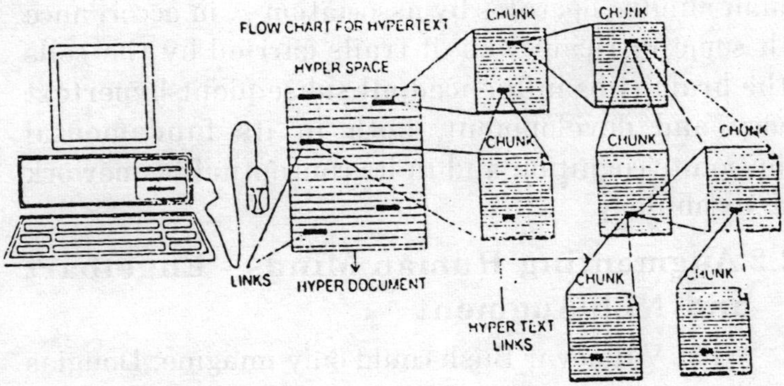

Fig. 11. Hypertext

the workings of the human mind. (See Jeffrey Conklin, OA Survey of Hypertext. *O IEEE Computer* 20, 1987, to which this or any other history of hypertext is indebted.)

5.2.1.Human Mind Operates by Association-Bush and Memex

While scholars continue to suggest forebearers of hypertext ranging from the Greeks to Sterne's *Tristram Shandy* and beyond, hypertext (although it was not called such until two decades later) has its roots in a single article ("As We May Think," *Atlantic Monthly* 176, 1945) by Vennevar Bush, then director of the United States Office of Scientific Research and Development. There Bush describes the "memex", a mechanical, microfiche-based, see-through desktop, "a device in which an individual stores .... books records and communications ... an enlarged intimate supplement to ... memory."

The memex, better suited to electronic and digital than to gear-driven information retrieval, was never built. Yet Bush's insistence that "the human mind ... operates by association ... in accordance with some intricate web of trails carried by the cells of the brain" has influenced all subsequent hypertext theory and development, both in its fundamental attention to cognition and in its conceptual framework and vocabulary.

5.2.2.Augmenting Human Minds - Engelbart and NLS/Augment

What Vannevar Bush could only imagine, Douglas Engelbart not only imagined but designed and built. In the process he invented or first put to serious use fundamentals of computer interaction, writing, and networking including word processing, outlining, windows, electronic mail, computer conferencing, collaborative authorship, and - not last - the mouse.

His 1962 paper, "A conceptual Framework for the Augmentation of Man's Intellect," (republished in Grief, ed., *Computer Supported Collaborative Work,* 1988) led to his development of a full-blown prototype hypertext system NLS (oNLineSystem) at the Science Research Institute in 1968. Renamed AUGMENT, this system was the beginning of Englebart's lifelong exploration into what he terms "a co-evolutionary process - new knowledge processes and new tools evolving together in real working environments.

5.2.3. Mind as Intertwingled "Docuverse" - Nelson and Xanadu

The last of the founding trinity of hypertext was also its baptizer. provocateur-humanist, Theodor Holm (Ted) nelson provide a utopian spirit and encompassing vision (as well as the coinage, hypertext, in the 1960's) to the new world off the mind imagined by Bush, and established by Engelbart.

Nelson is most likely also responsible for what George Landow has termed the "bizarrely celebratory" quality of writing about and with hypertext. Proceeding from a belief that "literature is an ongoing system of interconnecting documents." (*Literary Machines*, Edition 87.1, 2:2), Nelson has joyfully and wittily prophesied and proselytized the coming of a "docuverse" not unlike the linked world (as) text of contemporary computer networks. For decades Nelson has promised to embody the docuverse in his own Xanadu system, an ongoing design prospectus geared toward establishment of a peaceable kingdom of "intertwingled" and computerized text on earth (*Computer Lib/ Dream Machines*, Tempus Books, 1987).

5.2.5.Writing the mind -Bolter and Storyspace

It took the oddly fitting combination of a classicist and computer scientist to place hypertext both in its historical perspective as the successor to print and at the center of cultural scrutiny. Jay David Bolter's sometimes controversial *Writing Space* (referenced below) challenges assumptions of contemporary literary theory and computer science alike while making the case for hypertext as a new writing technology.

"Electronic writing is both a visual and verbal description," says Bolter, "not the writing of a place, but rather a writing with places, spatially realized topics .. sings and structures on the computer screen that have no easy equivalent in speech." For Bolter hypertext's "electronic symbols ... seems to be an extension of a network of ideas in the mind itself. "Storyspace, the hypertext system Bolter and I developed with John B. Smith, embodies Bolter's view that the "topographical" writing of hypertext "reflects the mind as a web of verbal and visual elements in a conceptual space."

5.2.6. Visions of Hypermedia

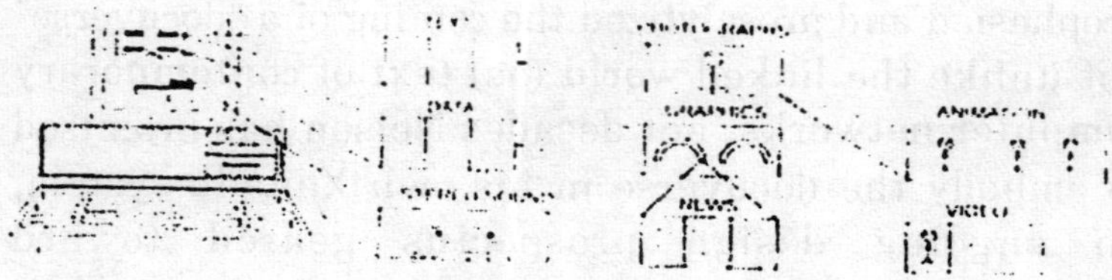

Fig. 12. Hypermedia

Hypertext has been called the revenge of the text on television since under its sway the screen image becomes subject to the laws of syntax, allusion, association and so on which characterize written language. Print literally gives way on hypermedia screens to digitized sound, animation, video, virtual reality, computer networks or databases which are linked to it. Thus images can be "read" as texts and vice-versa. Any hypertext holds the prospect of representing on the screen the sights, sounds and experience of movement through virtual worlds which language previously only evoked in the imagination.

5.2.7. Engelabart's Mouse Discovers Virtual Reality

By linking movements of the human hand with operations upon symbolic structures (words, windows, icons, etc.) on the computer screen, the electromechanical mouse, the now familiar interface device for which Douglas Engelbart holds a patent, opened the way to virtual reality (VR),. Virtual reality enacts continuously linked simulations within computer environments in response to body movements interpreted by the computer through input gleaned from "data gloves," special goggles or helmets, and the like.

While fully represented virtual reality as yet remains a costly research endeavor and entertainment enterprise, hypermedia simulations are regularly used in education, training marketing and entertainment. The design and storyboarding of these simulations likewise involves the use of hypermedia editing, presentation or desktop video tools. Graphical, "object-oriented" interface features, borrowed from CAD (Computer Aided Design) environments, script and create virtual worlds.

5.2.8. Continents of Knowledge from Fress to Intermedia

Windowed and interconnected worlds of knowledge now a commonplace of hypermedia (especially virtual reality) - owe of significant debt to a series of hypermedia systems developed at Brown University between 1968 and 1991. Hypertext pioneer Andries Van Dam, a graphics specialist, explored the development of multi-window systems, developing the Hypertext Editing System (HES) in 1968, quickly followed by FRESS (File Retrieval and Editing System). Not designed primarily for teaching, FESS was almost immediately used as the vehicle for networked instruction in a poetry course led by the critic Robert Scholes.

FRESS was followed by Intermedia, perhaps the most influential educational hypertext system in the brief history of hypertext. Members of Van Dam's research team, including Norm Meyrowitz, Nicole Yankelovich and Paul Kahn, were joined by Brown faculty members, most notably English Professor and hypertext theorist George P. Landow, in the development of Intermedia. "Webs," Van Dam's term for sets of hypertext links were incorporated into vast corpora ("continents of knowledge") of primary and secondary materials (including student commentaries) for courses in English, Biology and other disciplines. Landow's "concept maps" joined interactive graphical time-lines and web views as visual symbolic structures available to Intermedia learners. With Intermedia's demise in 1991, Landow transported his Dickens and In Memoriam (Tennyson) hypertext webs to Storyspace, publishing them as electronic textbooks and learning environments.

5.3. SHORT HISTORY OF HYPERTEXT

Table 11. Development of HT, HM, MM

1945	Vannevar Bush proposes *Memex*
1965	Ted Nelson coins the word *"hypertext"*
1967	The *Hypertext Editing System* and FRESS, Brown University, Andy van Dam
1968	Doug Engelbart demo of *NLS* system at FJCC
1975	*ZOG* (now KMS) : CMU
1978	*Aspen Movie Map*, first hypermedia videodisk, Andy Lippman, MIT Architecture Machine Group (now Media Lab)
1984	Filevision from Telos; limited hypermedia

database widely available for the Macintosh

1985 *Symbolics Document Examiner*, Janet Walker

1985 *Intermedia*, Brown University, Norman Meyrowitz

1986 OWL *introduces Guide*, first widely available hypertext

1987 Apple introduces *HyperCard*, Bill Atkinson

1987 *Hypertext'87* first major conference on hypertext

1991 *World Wide Web* at CERN becomes first global hypertext, Tim Berners-Lee

1992 *New York Times Book Review* cover story on hypertext fiction

1993 *Mosaic* anointed Internet killer app, National Center for Supercomputing Applications

1993 *A Hard Day's Night* becomes the first full-length feature film in hypermedia

1993 Hypermedia encyclopedias sell more copies than print encyclopedias

1995 Netscape Carp. gains market value of almost \$3G on first day of stock market trading "src="/share/images/icon.see-also.small.gif" WWW Consortium's list of hypertext projects

5.4. DEFINITIONS OF HYPERTEXT AND HYPERMEDIA

Test is an assembly of words, formed out of letters organized according to set of principles. We use text to communicate our ideas to others either by speech/talk or in written/printed form. Though we do not think linearly, while writing we try to join or link all those ideas in a logical manner. All written communications like books and other printed publications are linear, in which text is arranged sequentially. At the end there may be an index through which one can retrieve the information easily and quickly.

When text is converted into hypertext, all the individual idea instead of being joined sequentially will be linked in non-linear fashion with some logic. The information is stored in the nodal points, through machine generated links. This is considered to align more closely with human thinking than conventional computing.

The term 'hyper' refers to, over, in excess or exaggerated, while the term 'text' refers to, the main body of a book. The actual working of any written or printed. The subject of a discourse, a theme or topic. The term 'media' on the other hand refers to, 'medium' through which, such text, subject, discourse, theme, topic fully or part there are interlinked, integrated and retrieval.

HT consists of chunks or fragments of text, linked associatively. Nodes are the basic units of information in an HT. So, HT is creation and representation of links between discrete pieces of information (text or data). In HT, instead of continuous flow, text breaks into units or modules or fragments of information, which will be linked in non-sequential manner. In HM, more than one media are arranged in HT linking pattern.

Hypertext can be simply defined as non-sequential writing or as the text in electronic form that takes advantage of the interactive capabilities.

Hypertext is a method of for strong and retrieving data. Hypertext incorporates the notation of linking pieces of information allowing users to negative through network of chunks of information.

Hypermedia is simply the extension of HT that incorporates other media elements in addition to text With HM systems, authors can create linked corps of materials that include text, static and animated graphics, video, sound, music, etc.

HT document systems allow authors to link together any information blocks created with a text editor, while HM document systems provide linking capabilities between heterogeneous blocks created with different applications such as a painting program, chart package, or a music editor. In literature there are a number of definitions available, but most important ones are

1. **Hypertext :** Hypertext is non-sequential writing (Nelson 1965), 2, text in electronic form that takes advantage of the interactive capabilities is called Hypertext (Conklin 1987).
2. **Hypermedia :** Hypermedia is simply extension of Hypertext that incorporates other media elements in addition to text. With hypermedia system, authors can create corps of materials that includes text, static graphic, animated graphics, video sound, music, and so forth (Yankelovich 1988).

The deference between HT/HM is that HT systems allow authors to link together any textual information blocks. Which HM system provides linking capabilities between heterogeneous information blocks.

5.4.1. Hypertext and Print Media

Both HT and Print Media have established

their relative merits and demerits in their respective spheres. While paper as the source or medium of structuring and transforming information has been used for last several hundred years, HT, on the otherhand, is till in a state of cradle. The following are some of the distinguishing features normally notices between the HT on the one hand and the Print Media on the other

HT/HM	Print Media
(i) Major end-user benefits provided by HT organised databases are flexibility in browsing, access to small chunks of info, and review of information by used in least possible time;	(i) The user has to look several sources of printed versions requiring maximum time effort and even the required sources of info. May not be available at one place and at one point of time;
(ii) Difficult to use;	(ii) Easy to use;
(iii) To store heterogeneous formats of information on one platform/base would be difficult;	(iii) To store heterogeneous formats of information on one platform is easier and convenient;
(iv) Integrating comparing, and linking of two or more chunks/fragments of information is assured;	(iv) Integrating, comparing, and linking of two or more sets of information are difficult;
(v) The user of HT needs special training	(v) The user need no training;

5.5. CHARACTERISTIC OF HT AND HM SYSTEMS

1. In hypertext, information (text and dat) is represented in discrete chunks. The information may be paragraph, diagram, and graphics of image or a combination of any of these items.
2. An HT database is formed by interlinking chunks. A chunk could be linked with another or many chunks forming a network in the HT database.
3. Any document written by using HT technique is called a hyper document. In HT environment, the information chunks or frames will be linked within and in between the hyper documents.
4. In HT systems the user can navigate rapidly in either directions between nodes of the HT database. An HT user to access information by both associative and intutive routes, irrespective of the actual location of information, or for any visible database structure.
5. Users can create, edit and rearrange the chunks according to their needs. HT databases can have changeable structures, which can be changed according to the author's or designer's addition or editing of the text, graphics, images, etc. It does not have a clear structure like a conventional book in which the length, breadth, etc. can be defined.
6. AT any time reader/user is able to see only a small fragment of information from a large HT database.
7. There are no page boundaries as in a conventional book.

8. To a large extent, HT leaves control of information in the hands of users.
9. Unlike a printer book, HT is Multifaceted, with many entry points to add or retrieve information according to the need/requirement, level of interest and learning in style of the user population.

5.6. TYPES OF HYPERTEXT

Ted Nelson has classified Hypertext into five types :

5.6.1. Chunk or Discrete Style HT

It consists of separate pieces of text called 'chunks' which are connected by links and represented in the form of footnote markers. When the user interacts with the chunks, they come out with a response and present an entirely new fragment of information compared with traditional sequential form. While constructing this type of database, one has to provide these links logically, artistically and also according to the subject relevance, through which a reader can grasp, understand, and assimilate the knowledge easily.

5.6.2. Collateral HT

For two types of data structures, creation of collateral HT is possible. It may be useful to compare collateral equivalents of two tables of contents, writer's notes, etc. Creation multiple viewable links in between any two data structure is called 'collation' and the structures are called "collateral structures'.

5.6.3. Stretchtext

In stretchtext, the screen will show two 'throttles',

the first one moves the text forward and backward, up and down on the screen; the second throttle causes changes in the writing itself. This is completely controlled by the user. The text can also be changed with the throttles connected to the computer. Stretchtext can be made longer/shorter by adding and substracting words or phrases respectively.

5.6.4. Grand HT

It is consists of 'everything' written about a subject or relevant to it, tied together by editors, and the users can navigate in all the directions and read the information according to their choice. There are different pathways of thinking. Ted Nelson's Xanadu is the best example of grand hypertext system, in which one can read 'everything' and also write on the screen.

5.6.5. Specific HT

It is specifically written for a particular purpose in a specific area, consequently the usage also will be limited to specific type of clientele.

5.7. CLASSIFICATION OF HT AND HM SYSTEMS

We can classify the Hypertext and Hypermedia systems according to broad classification, environment or generations.

5.7.1. Broad Classification

Conklin has classified all the available hypertext systems into four types under the broad classification.

5.7.1.1. Macro Literary Systems

These systems are similar to very large size outline libraries in which all types of information on every topic will be stored an can be retrieved. The broad based systems like Memex, Augment, Xanadu and Textnet were designed for the multi-user environment, where one can store all types of published information. The could also be used for various purposes like publishing, reading, collaborative works and criticism.

5.7.1.2. Problem Exploration systems

These systems are basically issue-investigation type, designed to support high interactivity and unstructured thinking. They are developed to assist the members of a team in creating and structuring of information. These systems assist the users with such mechanisms by providing information lenses to filter the various levels of details. They also permit the user to see differing views of the same information.

5.7.1.3. Structure Browsing Systems

These systems are almost like systems described at, but smaller in size and are being used for computer-aided teaching, reference, and public information.

5.7.1.4. Modified Database Management Systems (DBMS)

Now-a-days a number of make DBMS packages are coming with simple HT linking features. To make DBMS software useful and attractive, the designers incorporate the flavor of HT technique, but they are not real HT systems. Normally we find such features in the currently used software for information retrieval purposes where data pointers merely increase text retrieval facilities. They are retrofit systems rather than true HT systems.

5.7.1.5. General Experimental Systems

There are a number of systems developed for experimentation of reading, writing, collaboration, etc aspects of HT such as a Intermedia, NoteCards and HyperCard. Even though they are strong in some aspects of HT, they are very general in nature and could be used for any work.

5.7.2. HT and HM Classification with Reference to Environment

5.7.2.1. Distributed Systems

Normally these systems are very large powerful and are able to handle very large volumes of information. Since they are multi-user systems, they allow a number of users to work at a time in doing collaborative work.

Intermedia is a good example for this type and is being used for computer-aided instruction, at the Brown University for the past three years.

5.7.2.2. PC-Based Systems

These are single user systems, comparatively small in size and could be used to design personal HT applications. The most popular example of this king HyperCard. Other include Guide, HyperTIES, and Link Way.

5.7.3. Classification Based on Generations

Despite the commonality in the basic architecture of the HM systems, they are classified into two generations. All the generation HM systems originally developed on mainframes, mainly focussed on text nodes and user display technologies with little or no graphics capabilities. However, they were developed to support work of a team, sharing a common HM network. These systems were developed prier to 1980 and include NLS/Augment, FRESS and ZOG.

These developed after 1980 are second generation systems which include various workstation based, research-oriented, and PC-based systems. The first category systems include NBoteCards. Nepture, Intermedia, Plain Text and KMS. These systems have go advanced three-dimensional graphics interface, strong support of graphics, animation composite multimedia nodes, sophisticated navigational displays and interface tailor ability. They were basically designed for single users or small teams of workers later PC based HT systems guide, HyperTIES, LinkWay, HyperPAD, HyperDOC etc have emerged.

5.8. APPLICATIONS OF HT AND HM SYSTEMS

These systems find applications in the following areas:

* Technical documentation for example, DE, ThothII
* Help systems, for example, Emacs, INFO, HyperCard, Guide, askSAM.
* Museum exhibits, for example. Kings Herald's Dream, for Jewish Heritage, HyperTIES.
* Religious studies, for example, The Bible library
* Problem solving and idea processing, for example, IBIS.
* Software engineering, for example, CASE, Neptune.
* Authoring and designing tools, for example, Hypercard, guide, HyperDoc.
* Collaborative writing, for example, WE, Notes.

* Writing aids, for example, HyperCard, HyperDoc, LSM InfoMaster, etc
* Computer-aided training/teaching CSILE, IRIS's INTERMEDIA
* Presentation aids and information koisks, for example, Boston MacWorld, LITA Conference Information Disk, Metacatolog (multilingual information kiosk)
* Information and retrieval system, for example, HIRS, Hyped, KRS, IBSI
* Library and information handling sources/services
  - Dictionaries, for example, OED, Webster's Dictionary
  - Encyclopedias, For example, Grolier's Electronic Encyclopedia, Compton's Multimedia Encyclopedia.
  - Medical text books, for example, Dynamic medical Handbook.
  - Product catalogues, for example, the Savings Zone Club Disk
  - Online user Manuals, for example, HyperCard.
  - Electronic maps, for example, HyperMap, Business Class
  - Travel guides, for example, Glasgow Online
  - Literary collections, for example, Xanadu Textnet
  - Electronic document publishing (considerable cost reduction in publishing, and distribution).
  - Expert Systems (+Hypertext), for example. Knowledge, Pulse, Hyper bridge, MacSmarts, 1st Class HT.

A number of American libraries are already using HT for Providing library and information services to their users. Apart from special and university libraries, a number of public libraries also started using HyperCard and other HT systems for providing services to the users of their libraries.

5.9. ADVANTAGES OF HT AND HM SYSTEMS

5.9.1. Ease of Tracing References

Machine support for link tracing means that all references are equally easy to follow forward to their referent, or backward to their reference.

5.9.2. Ease of Creating New References

Users can grow their own networks, or simply annotate someone else's document with the comment.

5.9.3. Information Structuring

Both hierarchical and non hierarchical organization can be imposed on unstructured information.

5.9.4. Customized Documents

Text segments can be threaded together in many ways, allowing the same document to serve multiple functions.

5.9.5. Modularity of Information

Since the same text segment can be referenced from several places, ideas can be expressed with less overlap and duplication.

5.9.6. Task Stacking

The user is supported in having several paths of inquiry active and displayed on the screen at the same time.

5.9.7. Collaboration

Several authors can collaborate, with the document and comments about the documents being tightly interwoven.

5.10. DRAWBACKS AND LIMITATIONS

5.10.1. Superficial Problems

Temporary in nature, these are implications or technological drawbacks, that are common to any new technology.

5.10.2. Deep Problems

These problems are stronger which may take long time to solve and sometimes they may not be solved at all. presently there are four such problems, which overlap each other.

5.10.3. Disorientation

The tendency to lose one's sense of location and direction in a nonlinear document.

5.10.4. Cognitive Overhead

The additional effort and concentration necessary to maintain several tasks or trails at one time.

5.10.5. Lack of Presentation Rhetoric

Indication of the destination of a link, and inviting the user to that destination are the two problems according to him. He has formulated nine rules for creating meaningful links in HT database to have logic or relationship among nodes. HT systems are useful only when there are balanced number of linear and nonlinear links; otherwise they lead to more distortion.

5.10.6. Construction of Default Paths

This problem is also related to rhetoric experienced in the construction of very bit HT databases. Construction of required links itself is a time consuming task and creating default paths requires more time. Thus this becomes a major constraint in designing a sophisticated HM system.

5.11. STORAGE AND DISTRIBUTION OF HT AND HM DOCUMENTS

The main problems in storage and distribution of HT and HM systems are their size and multimedia nature. Since these have graphics, photographs animation sound, etc they normally require very large disk space. Which often exceeds the memory of large computers also. For a simple HT system, memory of a microcomputer is adequate whereas the same will be inadequate for HM. In general, most of the HM systems require an external storage device for storing and usage. Some of the storage and distribution devices include magnetic disks, videodisks, optical disks, and online networks or bulletin board systems.

5.12. HYPERTEXT MARKUP LANGUAGE

HTML is a Hypermedia document description language used to publish document on the WWW.HTML documents are written in plaintext (ASCII) with the file extension (htm). There are a number of ways to create an HTML document: Any editor may be used and the HTML commands may be used and the HTML commands may be added in. A HTML editor that inserts the commands in the appropriate locations may be used. Further, a conversion utility that takes a document from some other format and converts it to HTML may be used.

5.11.1. HTML Document Tags:<HTML>, <HEAD>,<BODY>:

HTML uses <HTML>,<HEAD>,<BODY> as the document tags. Several tags to documents but do not affect the presentation of the documents but convey important information to the browsers and the users. The document should have corresponding. </ HTML,<HEAD,>/BODY> tags respectively at the end. HTML is not case sensitive.

5.11.2. Markup Tags

Like many word processing systems, HTML allows to define the structure of a document as we specify such things as lists, titles, headings, and so on. The markup tags in details are as below :

5.11.2.1. Title: <TITLE>

A title succinctly describes the content of the document.

5.11.2.2. Heading:<HEADING>

These are header tags, for headings. In HTML there are different header tags: <H1>, <H2>, <H3>, <H4>, <H5>, <H6>, <H1> is the largest and prominent header while <H6> is the smallest one.

5.11.3. Paragraphs : <P>

The <P> specifies a paragraph break. It does not require end tag. If the not include in the any <P> HTML text, it will appear as one long paragraph, </ P> is used to end paragraph.

5.11.4. Lists

HTML provide several ways to display information in lists. These include.

Uinnumbered lists	UL>[LIST]</UL>
Numbered lists	<OL>[LIST]</OL>
MENU LISTS	<ENU>[LIST]>/MENU>
Directory LISTS	<DIR>[LIST]</DIR>
Definition lists	DL>[LIST]</DL>

5.11.5. Preformatted text: <PRE>

When one does not want the web browser to change the formatting of plain text, preformatted text is used

5.11.6. Long Quotations : <BLOCK QUOTATIONS>

To make long quotations in document.

5.11.7. Line Break :

It simply forces a line break in the text. Unlike the <p> tag, an extra line not inserted.

5.11.8. Address : <ADDRESS>

Used to mark addresses. Typically, it occurs at the end of documents, and is used to enclose the author's name and electronic main addresses. By default it comes in italics.

5.11.9. Comments : <!->

Text appearing within comment tags will be ignore by browsers, it cannot be nested within one another.

5.12. SOME TIPS CREATION OF THE HTML DOCUMENT

1. Divide the documents into head and body parts.
2. Do not forget closing tags.
3. Never use more than one title in a document.

4. Never use other tags in a title
5. Keep the title fairly short-not more than 64 characters.
6. Make the titles meaningful
7. When nesting lists, do not forget to close each list with the appropriate tag
8. Avoid HTML tags in comment fields - it is not a good idea to place portions of your document in a comment field to try to prevent it from being displayed.
9. Browsers do not always handle tags within comment fields correctly
10. Look at your document in more than one browser. Different browsers may display the same elements in dissimilar ways.

There is no doubt that HT has created a new revolution and opened a new way of presenting the information. At the same time, many people, especially computer scientists, believe that HT concept is a breakthrough, in the computer world; something comparable to the invention of printing machine. HTML has the intrinsic advantage of providing links to images sound and video files through the use of simple tags. With the onset of Internet, web pages-that include the elements of hypermedia has been designed.

REFERENCES

1. Srivath, M and Bagavathi., Hypertext methodology for knowledge organization. **In** : Satyanarayana, B.Ed., *Information Technology : Issues and Trends.* Vol. 1 New Delhi : COSMO, 1998. PP 157-163.
2. Ramaiah, C.K., Hypertext and hypermedia : An overview. In : *DESIDOC Bulletin of Information Technology*, Vol.

12(6), 1992, PP 3-5.

3. Nelson, Theodor. H., Computer library/dream machines Microsoft, Redmond, 1984.
4. Ramaiah, C.K., **Op cit.**, PP 4.
5. Panda, K.C., and Gautam, J.N., In'fo Technology on the Crossroad : From Ab'acus to Internet, Agra : Y.K., 199. PP 156-170.
6. Shewale, N.G. and Panigrahi, P.K., Hypertext and HTML tools and techniques to develop web pages. **In :** *Library Science with slant to Documentation and Information Studies.* Vol. 34(3), 1997. PP 151-.
7. Ramaiah C.K., hypermedia systems and their applications in education. **In :** Cnand, K. ed., *Perspectives of multimedia : Media information services in India,* New Delhi : Batra, 1996. PP 34-42.
8. Ramaiah, C.K. **Op cit,.** PP 4-8.
9. **Ibid.**, PP 4-8.
10. Feldman, Tony., The Multimedia, London : Blueprint, 1999. 67-69.
11. Shewale, N.G. and Panigrahi, P.K., Op cit., 152-156.
12. **Ibid.**, PP 1-56.

6

Multimedia

The present century has been a revolution in Information Technology all over the world. Computers are playing an increasing vital role, touching upon every aspect of our day-to-day life. The PC industry is at the central stage of existing integration process, which will merge both personnel and computing industries with a telecom, electronic media, entertainment industries, education and library services, resulting a total revolution in presenting storing and retrieval of information.

The key role for information centres and libraries (LIC) in education and research demands that they must harness information technology (IT) to encourage the library users to make better use to traditional information resources and to develop new methods to access the information through verities of services for attracting a wide range of users. Librarians are in a position to meet the challenges, and provide the information resources to the users with the help of ITs without any fear, frustration and failure.

Consequently these trends pave the way for

new development opportunity with its focal point being multipurpose PC plat form or Multimedia (MM). The deployment of MM system enables us for the first time to mix the information from a variety of sources. Using the medium from most appropriate means like Video, audio animation and text etc. within a single digital environment.

6.1. MEANING AND DEFINITIONS

The term 'multimedia' is relatively a technology concept both in art and technology. It is true we can say that multimedia is a fruit of this decade. Earlier to this decade most of us were laymen to the multimedia. The word multimedia has been used in the computer industry since mid 1980s. In the present days multimedia is just like a red rose that dissolves into a little girl's face when you press "Valentine's day".

Simple multimedia is the combination of multi-medium, "multi" means many of more than two and "media" is the plural form of medium. Multimedia can be defined as, `an integration of several media such as, text, audio, video, graphic, animation etc.[1]. In the computer society, multimedia refers to the programme that uses more than one method for communication to the users. There is different meaning for different people on MM Technically, "to illustrate the text information on the computer screen with the audio system is an example of MM"[2]. Some of the commonly available MM products are videodisks, videotapes, CD-ROM, Sound Blaster, TV etc.

Medium can be referred to storage, transmission, communication, representation, presentation, input interaction and perception, means that it can refer to different levels of abstraction. It is also refers to a basic information type like text, graphics, image, video or audio. MM can be defined as, an integration of several media, etc.[3].

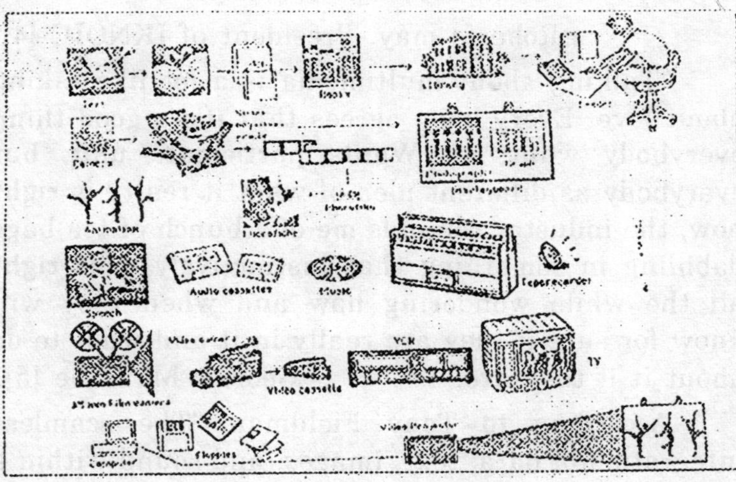

Fig. 13. Multimedia

Generally multimedia is fusion of computing with audio-video technology. In other words computer software which includes the following:

Text : May be tabie of contents to entire novels.

Data : May be a statistics table, charts, graphs.

Spread sheets : Ledger and others

Audio : May be human voice, music, sound effects etc.,

Graphics : May be drawings, paintings. prints maps blue prints etc.,

Still pictures : Slides, Transparencies. negatives and others.

Animation : Covers a vast range of creative

technology and media from three-dimensional figures to computer-generated figures.

Moving pictures : Moving photographic images.

"We defined multimedia as any thing that request more than two trips to the car".

- Roberts may. President of IKNOIC [4].

"Talking about multimedia is a lot like taking about love. Every body agrees that it's a good thing everybody wants it. Wants participate unit, but everybody as different idea of what it realty is right now, the industry reminds me of a bunch of tea bags dabbling in something that instinctively feels right all the while wondering how and when they will know for sure if they are really in it and what to do about it if they are. - Georgic Mc Cabe [5].

According to Tony Fieldman "The scamless integration of data, text, images, and sound within a single, digital information environment and providing access to the stored information using computer systems which are user friendly and above all interactive"[6].

According to Waring Partridge "Multimedia as the integrated use of two or more media. Meaning in every day terms, the simultaneous communication of voice pulse handwriting data fax and video images"[7].

According to Michael Sullivan. Jr "Multimedia incorporates still and full motion video pictures, voices music and other sounds and a variety of touch based devices to help us to interact"[8].

To give background to the question of definition, a definition that given at the UIMS Workshop, Portugal, June 1990 is quoted below:

1. Multi-media is concerned with both input and output (including their combination called interaction).
2. For output, multi-media is concerned with multiple streams operating in parallel. Stream may not be the best word-channel, tracks or modes are alternatives.
3. For input, Multi-media is concerned with simultaneous input events generated by one or several different devices all being used parallel.
4. On input, it is concerned with the composition of higher level input tokens in term of primitive events[9].

6.2. MULTIMEDIA ITS ORIGIN

MM is not a new mechanism, It was developed with the extension of Hypertext and Hypermedia technology. Hypertext document system allows users to link together any information, where as hypermedia is similar to HT, but instead of linking text, user can link to other media *i.e.* graphics, video, audio and animation tee. The concept of hypertext was originated but Dr. Vannevar Bush for the first time in 1945, when he was science adviser of Roosevelt President of USA. During those days he foresaw the problem of future information explosion and developed a mechanical recording device which he called "MEMEX" for his information needs. During 1950 Douglas C. Engelbart a computer scientist picked up the idea and developed a system called" On line system"(NLS) Which later named as AUGMENT (text processing multi-user system). In 1965 Theodore H. Nelson coined the work "Hyptertext" and disseminated the idea to the world.

The modem definition of HT as "A large number of information fragments/chunks (such as text, graphics and images) linked together electronically forming a multifaceted indefinite shaped database in which one can write and read the information non sequentially and nonlinearly". In 1967 Nicholas Negroponte formed the architecture machine group in the Architecture Dept at MIT. It was when the MIT media Laboratory was established to develop multimedia system. After 1985 MIT media Lab took nearly 10-MM research projects and many other like Olivertti Research Lab 2 Apple Computer, Sony and Microsoft, Creative Lab of USA etc., are best company for developing MM applications.

One of the first and useful MM packages is Farallon Computing's media tricks which could be used to record a series of screens and use the sound hardware to record a step by step guide for using any Mac software. P-DOC is a software environment for electronic documentation, authoring and consultation based on HM. Mammal was developed by National Geographical Society and IBM Co. which provides information on 200 manual species which includes colour photographs, maps, animal-movements and sound etc. MULTIMEDIA consists of the integration of digital audio, video graphics, animation and text on computers. Interactive multimedia has come of age with the advent of the CD-ROM, a high capacity, inexpensive and sturdy storage medium.[10].

6.3. HISTORICAL DEVELOPMENTS

In the context of MM, it is important to emphasize that the MM approach is based on the new visions about the usage of the computers. It all started with the vision of Dr Vannevar Bush in 1945, reporting in his famous article "As we may think", where he described a new kind of computer tool, that should enable the user to link documents, notes, drawings, text sketches, photographs, etc. according to their needs implemented by Doug Engelbart, 15 year later in order to provide a set of tools for extending the human intellect. His goal was to design tools that enhance the capacities of the users using them, rather than develop systems replacing a limited intellect. The next milestones in this development were Theodore H. Nelson's vision about global HT Library 1965 and Bills Atkinson's vision about HT capacities for the ordinary user, realized in the form of HyperCard "Supercard", and similar products.

It can be concluded that MM/HM/HT was conceived in 1945, born in the 1960's, and slowly nurtured in 1970s and finally entered in the real world in 1980s with its rapid growth in 1985, culminating in a fully established field during 1989. Now, several real-world systems are available, that anybody can buy and store in their local computers [11,12].

6.4. A MULTIMEDIA REVOLUTION

In 1985, Microsoft called Multimedia" the new papyrus". There is another definition of multimedia usually spoken of in the same breath as the "information superhighway".

This involves the merging of communications media industries such as telephone, cable television, and movies companies. It is a vision of a network that will bring multimedia software -a and assorted other services-into the home through a cable. This vision is fast becoming reality as interactive services start to appear.

However you define it, multimedia is having a huge impact on our lives. It might have been premature to label it "the new papyrus" as Microsoft did a decade ago, but few now doubt that multimedia technology is set to play an equally revolutionary role.

6.5. DIGITAL DAYS

The key to this multimedia revolution is digitization, which means the conversion of all types of information, such as words, sound, pictures, video, and numbers, into a special code that electronic machines can recognize and understand.

The first type of machine to make use of digital information was the compute" "information processors", which filled whole rooms, began to appear in large organizations in the 1650s; they were used to performs complex calculations, and could display only text and figures on screen.

Soon, simple digital graphics were appearing on computers; inevitably, the first programs to be run on the graphics-capable systems were games.

Technology moved on, and by the late seventies, video arcades were offering interactive multimedia that combined graphics and computer generated should in games such as Space Invaders.

Soon hobbyists were buying the first home computers and games consoles. Then, in 1981, IBM unveiled its first PC (personal computer), and the business world bought into computing wholesale. Few people, however, predicted the breakneck pace of growth and development that has characterized the computer industry ever since.

Today about anything can be converted into digital code. A computer simply processes numbers and does not know or care whether those numbers represent a Mozart symphony, a Rembrandt self-portrait, or an accounting firm's five-year business plan. Multimedia home computers can now produce stunning 3-D graphics, photo-realistic pictures, movie footage, hi-fi sound, and breathtaking animation, while all the time they are just pushing figures.

Today's Multimedia computers are at the forefront of a much bigger multimedia revolution however; they are leading the move away from analog media machines towards digital ones.

6.5.1. Analog into Digital

Now-a-days most of the media machines at homes-such as TV sets, video records, radios, and most telephones are analog. They deal with information that has been transmitted as varying electrical voltages, not as electronic code.

This is changing fast, some cordless and cellular telephones already use digital technology. Radio stations are testing out digital broadcasting and the VCR (Video Cassette Recorder) is under threat form digital video, and so, while the thought of connecting your telephone to your TV set or your computer to your VCR may seem absorb now, one day they may all be in the same box. As the digitization of media proceeds space, and as the technology advances, so the foundations of the multimedia revolution are being laid.

At the forefront of progress is the CD, which was invented to hold digital music, but one, as the CD-ROM, carries multimedia information.

6.5.2. CD-Rom Delivers

CD-ROM sprang directly form the music CD, and form the same set of parents-Sony and Philips. It is a logical step; after all music CDs store a stream of electronic code that represents sound waves, Replace that code with one that conveys digital pictures, text animation, and so on, attach a modified CD player to a computer, and you have CD-ROM.

When CD-ROM first appeared in the mid-1980s, the storage capacity is offered the computer world seemed truly awesome. It could hold about 20 times more information than the hard dick of a typical desktop computer. To put that into perspective, a single CD-ROM has been so successful a way to deliver multimedia. In fact. CD-ROM has been so successful a way to deliver multimedia products that now no home computer can be called truly complete without a CD-ROM drive [12,14,15,16].

6.6.3. Multimedia CDs:

Multimedia products use a combination of text, graphics, video and sound to present its information content. Apart form Indian users these CDs are useful for non-Indians as well as NRSs for knowing Indian culture, languages, etc. Publications like mystica India and Karishma give an interesting account of popular beliefs, customs, and practices, ceremonies and rituals that pervade the daily lives of most Indians. There are also full of fun, games, and puzzles, apart from 200 B C to the present. This would help the second generation of Bengali NRIs to learn about Bengal.

All about Sikhism and on Guru Granth sahib includes the teachings of Sri Guru Nanak in the original script of Gurumukhi and translations in Punjabi and English. This product would be very useful these who like know about Sikhism.

Similarly products are available on Jainsim, Buddhism, Christianity and also Mahabaratha on CD. And also CD-ROM on Vedic math's and great personalities like Mahatma Gandhi Interesting CDs are available on subjects like vas5tu Sastra, Aksharadham etc [17].

6.5.4. Hardware (C.P.U.)

PC-286 or 386 Processor at least 4 MB Ram (8 MB is preferable)

VAG Graphics

Digital audio System

HD 80 MB (120 MM is preferable)

VHS-VCR controller card (8 bits is acceptable, but 16 is preferable)

A CD-ROM drive (at least 150 K per second transfer rate)

Audio-Amplifier/speaker

Any model right form PC-286 to PC-386 can be shown as per requirements.

IT is not essential to have CD-ROM drive, video card, etc., but these may also be added if the application demands for it.

6.5.5. Software

Authority Software (e.g. Windows, Linkway,

Authorware, Professional) Micro Minicard, etc. [18].

6.5.6. Multimedia Packages

With the growing popularity of multimedia technology in library circles. The numbers of multimedia packages are increasing at an alarming rate. Some of the popular packages are:

1	Asymetrix Multimedia tool book	4.0
2	Microsoft Visual Basic	2.0
3.	Macromedia director	5.0
4.	Oracle Media objects	1.0
5.	Strate Media Forge	2.0

6.6. COMPONENTS OF MULTIMEDIA

Usually there are five components in MM software, the four of which are text, graphics, animation and sound, the fifth component being, interactive links that integrate the whole program by giving the user a way to interact with the program and cause things to happen. An exposition of the these components is detailed below:

6.6.1. Text

Text is mostly available in printed documents in different forms viz., full text, bibliographic indexes, etc. Text is the base for word processing programs and is the fundamental information used in most of the MM programs. In fact, MM packages often involve the conversion of book (full text) to computerized form. Allowing the user to look up information quickly (without constantly referring to an index of contents).

6.6.2. Graphic Images

Graphic images generally mean a "still" image

viz., photographic, online drawing or graphs (bar, linear, circular, etc.) and play an important role in the presentation of data of any R&D work. For any human being, visually oriented materials and pictures are a powerful means to illustrate information whether on a piece of paper or on the computer screen. Graphic images are, therefore, an important component of MM. A hospital's database of patients with names, addresses and other information is much more effective if the photographs of those patients (including X-rays, anatomical structure if disease etc.) can be displayed. Graphic files are always larger and occupy more storage space in computer than the text files. This is one of the reasons why MM applications require hard disk drive or equivalent storage capacities, such as CD-ROM.

6.6.3. Animations

Like graphic images, animations refers to a moving picture or videos, and are also powerful communicators and useful for illustrating concepts that involve movement. These concepts are difficult to illustrate using a single photograph or even a series of photographs, and even more difficult to explain using text and helps in varieties of decisions. Animation files require much more storage space than graphic files involving a single image. This often necessities the uses of a CD-ROM drive.

6.6.4. Sound

Sound can substantially reinforce our understanding of information presented in other ways. Inclusion of sound in MM program serves as a more powerful and useful tool to provide information to users which otherwise is not possible using any other method.

6.6.5. Interactive links

Interactive nature is an integral part of MM. This means that the user can point with a mouse and click on certain screen "objects" such as, button or highlighted text and cause the programme to respond in a certain way. It is the interactive nature of the MM that takes care of every thing to provide information to users.

6.7. FEATURES OF MULTIMEDIA

6.7.1. Multimedia

It includes many media such as text, photos, sound, graphics, animation, video, etc, combined media is more effective for teaching than single medium.

6.7.2. Interactivity

Multimedia computer technologies allow the learner to participate and the technology respond to the learner's choice in an interactive way.

6.7.3. Self-paced learning

Multimedia programs have detailed instructions for self-directed learning. People can learn more easily when they can see, hear and work with new technologies.

6.7.4 Ease of use

Multimedia packages are generally easy to use is they are designed/developed even for learners with little or no prior knowledge.

6.7.5 Audio

Audio is the 'front end' of a multimedia system. It comprises an audio adapter, an audio input devices such as microphone, software to digitize the analog sound, amplifiers and speakers.

6.7.6 Video

Video is the major 'front end'. Rapid advances in video digitization technology have enable video to be harnessed and developed on the desktop. Real-time video delivery, that is, delivering the presentation 'live' requires a high-speed, high-bandwidth network. Today, real time video feeds such as those by the Cable Nets Network (CNN) can be viewed on the desktop.

6.7.7 Virtual Reality (VR)

These applications are programmes that could envelop a user with a 3-D simulated environment of sight, movement, sound and possibly touch in the future.

6.8. USE OF MULTIMEDIA

Multimedia has found use in

1. Community information.
2. Corporate section information system.
3. Education and training.
4. Geographical information systems.
5. Home shopping and entertainment.
6. Language training.
7. Management training.
8. Multimedia main facility.
9. Personal and global information system.

10. Reference and information sources [19,20,21,22].

6.8.1. Multimedia V/s Hypermedia

Students of Information technology are often confused with the conceptual distinctions of these two near synonymous terms "multimedia and "Hypermedia" a subject of Hypermedia has simplified. The utilization of a vast amount of information to a considerable extent. The basic differences between are, however, as under:

Table 12. Differences between hypermedia and multimedia

Hypermedia	*Multimedia*
1. An extension of the concept of hypertext to include pictures, sound movies, and so on, along with text and links, to other documents.	1. Multimedia form of communication combining text with graphics page-layout, motion pictures sounds animation, and so on.
2. Hypermedia is a subst of hypertext.	2. Multimedia a subset of hypermedia.

6.9. INFUSION IT LIBRARIES SERVICES

Future historian will remember the last half of the 20th century as the dawning of the age of information. A big question today is how information can be used to make better plans and decision in business, government, and the R&D works or even in personal matters. Thus information processing has become a major social activity now, more than 75% typical executive's time spent in processing some type of information. The libraries and library processionals of today need to shoulder the responsibility of managing the information explosion by adaptation of latest IT. The library manager need not sit as a spectator; in turn they must ensure the best use of IT by critically assessing and by considering the needs of their organization as a trendsetter and status seeker. So the "future library has to move from the store house of knowledge to a plat form for generation, exchange and utilization of knowledge", and the library professionals must be capable of providing any type of information in any format currently available in the IT society. Multimedia is no longer a futuristic technology, which is not available now but also affordable. The kind of results till now a dream could be achieved through MM from all point view education, training, research, publishing, advertising, games, home shopping audio, video, production for information storage and retrieval etc. Thus MM is a unique development both for library staff the user.

6.10. APPLICATIONS OF MULTIMEDIA

Multimedia systems are being used for many purposes by different people in different organizations/ officers/environment. The main functions include media integration, storing, organization and dissemination at different places in different ways. This paper attempted in reviewing the use of multimedia for library and information services in various countries from the published literature. Some of general applications of multimedia are given below:

1. Instruction/training and technical presentations.
2. Multimedia communications such as multimedia

Fig. 14. Multimedia applications in libraries

e-mail, personal conferencing, video phones, video conferencing, etc.

3. Public information point/kiosks for libraries musecums, hospitals; tourists, sites. monuments, etc.
4. Medical information systems.
5. Multimedia databases, multimedia information banks.
6. Multimedia newsletters, multimedia books, other information resources.
7. Reference tools, e.g. encyclopedias, dictionaries etc.
8. Archival systems.
9. Geographical information systems.
10. Electronic publishing & bookselling.
11. Point-of-sale displays.
12. Product information catalogues.
13. Technical documentation, including engineering, drawings, specifications, etc.

14. Architectural information displays for example walk-through programmes for the new buildings or constructions/already constructed buildings/ mounments.
15. Entertainment, leisure, homes.
16. Exhibitions such as conferences, trade shows new product, facilities, museums, libraries, etc.
17. Interactive displays in museums, hospitals, libraries, etc.

Tourism is one of the industries that have exploited the full strength of multimedia for developing tourist information systems for public libraries.

6.11. MULTIMEDIA APPLICATIONS IN LIBRARIES

MM system is enables us for the first time to mix the information from the verity of sources using the medium most appropriate to the message as video clip, Computer animation, or screen full of text and sound effects as needed. One can select any away as per his requirement in a key stroke or the user can point with a mouse and click on certain screen "objects" and cause the programme to respond in a certain away.

MM have a wide area importance on the library point of view, which can be, judge by its following usefulness.

1. It allows the user to brows and navigate quickly any type of complex information.
2. It has optimum freedom for the user.
3. If offers innumerable possibilities for teaching and learning any subject with any modification mode.

4. It single form could serve the purpose of the different levels of users.
5. Resource sharing/networking or some of the most important features of MM.
6. It creates 3-D effects in variety of ways of any object.
7. It can be single stand-alone system or multi-user system.
8. The uses find the programmes are interesting and excellent. It made the entire system, easy and quick. It given the ability to handle live and stored system, easy and quick. It gives the ability to handle live and stored data simultaneously to user with new kinds of devices.
9. It is interesting and easy to use over the exiting form such as print, microforms, online, etc.
10. It controls and interactivity helps the users and provides the benefits of books (information) and human beings (interactivity).
11. It can help satisfying different information needs such as reference, enrichment, entertainment, leisure, etc.
12. It can help meeting various types of information preferences of the users such as scholarly, scientific, vocational, artistic recreational, etc.

Electronic information, and multimedia in general, is about to become a vital part of our cultural heritage. Libraries have throughout the history ensured a democratic, independent and free access to the knowledge and intellectual value represented by conventional books. It is evident that this principles is also valid for electronic information and multimedia. The availability of multimedia information through data networks may also open completely new ways for the libraries to obtain information for the common users.

6.12. AMERICAN AND EUROPEAN LIBRARIES

Many big libraries including the Library of Congress (LC), British Library, OCLC, etc are building their collections in multimedia form. Apart from multimedia collection development in 1990, LC began the American Memory Project, aided by Annenberg Fund; the David and Lucile Packard Foundation; and others, for preparing multimedia CDs. This conversed several kinds of information including country's historical books, pamphlets. Photographs, folk songs, movies, genealogical works, etc.

LC brought out the first part of this project America at the start of a New Century 1880-1920, as a CD. Similarly, Elmer E Rasmussen Library and University of Alaska started a Project Jukebox-a HyperCard based Multimedia Archival system. Project Jukebox is used for Archiving as well as providing access to recordings of oral history archives.

For the past five years, many libraries in the developed countries started various projects such as archiving different forms of information, multimedia databases, multimedia catalogues, walk-through programmes, Instructional packages, electronic books, and digital libraries. There are a few surveys in the literature that focused on the usage of multimedia technology in public libraries, academic libraries and special libraries. These studies primarily cover the use of multimedia CD-ROMs in libraries and also the use of World Wide Web and Internet.

6.13. INDIAN SCENARIO

Now a day many libraries feel that the multimedia should be integrated into the regular services by the libraries. Even in advanced countries, libraries do not have a separate department or personnel responsible for multimedia products or services. For the past 2-3 years, use of electronic resources, particularly multimedia ·in libraries has improved considerably, However, budget for multimedia products still seems to be less, but it is growing for bigger libraries situated in metropolitan cities.

Generally for selecting multimedia products, libraries depend on retail stores displays, publisher's catalogues, reviews, advertisements, trade shows, demos, computer magazines and catalogues. The main type of multimedia products being sought in libraries are reference and educational. Other related categories include databases, electronic books, software and their training packages entertainment, leisure, etc.

Most of the libraries are using multimedia resources for reference service and instructional purpose. In this connection, a survey was undertaken by the author on the use of multimedia in Delhi libraries to have a clear picture of usage in Indian libraries particularly in Delhi. So far published results are not available in the literature. Overall, in spite of cost reduction in the multimedia hardware and software, use of the multimedia resources in limited to some of the national level institutions or organizations.

However, the majority of the libraries are now setting up such facilities for their users. After the availability of internet in a very large scale in the offices, libraries, and houses, multimedia has become more popular, with the result most of the decision makers/financial authorities are realizing the importance of multimedia in the daily life and particularly in libraries.

American Centre Library, British Council Libraries and a few other libraries in Delhi are having good number of multimedia PCs (MPCs) for using Internet and Multimedia Resources to their users.

6.13.1. Application and Research on Multimedia Development on India

Though multimedia is still in an embryonic state, its popularly among, the Indian users and its, entry into the library market is not logging for behind. Some of the institutions those who have already can be tabulated as under to make our concept clearer.

6.14. LIMITATIONS OF MULTIMEDIA

Even though Multimedia systems have many advantages introducing, such systems into offices, schools, colleges, universities, libraries and homes is not easy task. Some observations are made with the introduction of Mm in the libraries:

1. **Technological :** Problems related to the company products its compatibility, control, strategy, standardization, copyright etc.
2. Skill : Before using the user should have take training when and where they need it in the library. It requires trained personnel.
3. **Concentration :** These databases are generally

Table 13 : Institutions experimenting multimedia

Sr No.	*Name of the Institution*	*Area of which Multimedia experiment is being conducted*
1.	NIC-New Delhi	IR related Activities
2.	C-DAC, Pune	Biomedicine for medical utilization
3.	NECERT, New Delhi	Teaching and learning research techniques
4.	PBL company in join collaboration with sony and Microsoft	Production of Video on demand terminal for domestic use
5.	KCC software Ltd., New Delhi, in collaboration with front Line center pty, Australia	Computer based solution and Support in school education
6.	Oracle Software, India Ltd.	Media Products and services to provide saleable MM library services.
7.	Apple computer Inc/Apple Development India, B'lore	On MM software
8.	NIIT, New Delhi, Calcutta, Bombay, and Bangalore.	On MM software
9.	Creative Technology, USA and Singapore/Matrox and Fast Electronics, German with India Venders	On MM products like CD-ROM. Sound and laser, video Blaster work station, and Networking Products.

very large and the new user finds it difficult to keep control of it. Therefore an additional effort and concentration is required by the user.

4. **Physical strain** : IT causes lot of physical strain on reader's eyes and brain, for which this is nit so popular.
5. **Suitable MM Configuration** : There may not be single agency to cater to the needs of our objects of assimilating a MM System.

6.15. TYPES OF MULTIMEDIA SYSTEMS

6.15.1. Multimedia Library Information kiosks/walk through programmes

Improving accessibility to both collections and services has always been a concern of libraries. Several libraries made attempts to create plans and guides to help users. In this connection, multimedia is one of the best tools for creating electronic library guides or web library guides or electronic tours for their users. Many libraries in the US and Europe have started using hypermedia for designing library walk-through programs for their users.

Reference service is one of the most visible services that can be provided by these systems. In one study, it was found that 44 percent of reference questions were directional, 18 per cent were instructional, 32 per cent actual reference and 6 per cent were extended reference. In another study, it was found that 34 per cent of the queries are actual reference and 66 per cent are directional. So, Librarians designed Hypermedia Library Information Kiosks for their users to provide quick reference and redeployed the reference staff in other library activities.

Some other important examples of multimedia library guide web library guides/electronic tours are:

(a) Electronic Library Guide in the University of Birmingham's main library, created using Took Book.

(b) Guide to South Bank Universit's Centenary Library, developed with HyperCard.

(c) Multimedia Database of Tourist Information developed using HyperCard by the Public Library of Gateshead Libraries and Arts Service

6.15.2. Instruction/Training

The role of multimedia in instruction has been well documented in several research experiments done in various disciplines. So, librarians have started using multimedia as a tool to train their staff in the new library technologies/applications and also to the users to provide training about using library resources. The main advantage of using multimedia for training is its interactivity, hence, it is being used by several schools, colleges, and universities for designing individualized library instructional packages for providing training to their users and also to provide in-depth subject training to their staff.

The training programme covers library services, online catalogue, orientation to the libraries, circulation policy, access to journals literature, preservation of library materials, introduction to reference work, using e-mail, technical services, integrated online systems for libraries, and acquisition and processing library materials. A few multimedia-based CAI packages designed using HyperCard used for library staff training/instruction are:

* Illuminate-a Multimedia-based CAI project about the University of Minnesota Library's OPACs
* Tour of the Internet-a quick tour about the Internet
* Information Access-a library research skills tutorial for the university students
* HyperCard-based AACR2 - a self teaching CAI package for preparing catalogue cards
* HyperCard-based University of Hawaii OPAC tutorial
* Cat Skills-an interactive Multimedia package to teach AACR2. It is a good professional training tool for students, beginners in cataloguing and working librarians. This multimedia CD is available in both Mac and Windows platforms. The Library Association, London is marketing this tool for 495 pounds
* UGE 100 Library Skills-designed by the Wayne State University Library
* Teaching Mini Medline-a training tool for library users
* STAR (Students Tutorial Access & Resources) - CAI package designed for OSU Libraries
* Hypermedia-based CBT package for training the new staff of University of Tennessee, Knoxville libraries.

6.15.3. Self Learning Tools

For people who need practical education in areas such as home ownership, vehicles repairing, etc, the multimedia CD-ROMs are a good medium for presenting the nuts-and-bolts tasks required to keep the house/machine functioning. For example, the house repair Encyclopedia provides a thorough compendium of well-illustrated repair guidelines, covering essential tasks such as stopping water leak, performing electrical wiring, pouring concerete, fixing a roof and patching the damaged walls and ceilings. Individual tasks are depicted in animation, sound, video and providing far better information than the static pages of a book.

The Internet Resource Guide is an online book about Internet that describes the various services available on it. Similarly many more commercial multimedia self-learning tools are available in the market. Some of the important training applications available in libraries are National Geographic's Animal Samplings, ABC Golf, Music Data City, Cartoon Jukebox (an interactive coloring book for children) and Magic Flute, etc. These are self learning tools that any library can purchase and provide free education/instruction to their library users.

6.15.4. Digital/Electronic Libraries

Digital libraries are basically decentralized and easily extensible able to support interpretability between tools, applications and systems; support heterogeneity both in terms/forms of data and systems tools supported; able to support a rich information seeking environment; and scaleable in terms of the size of the system. Digital information may include digital books, scanned images, graphics, data digitized A-V clips, etc.

It is scaleable storage and network management system that allows libraries to grow without sacrificing the convenience of anytime, anywhere access, it also provides a hierarchical storage system to protect the assets from loss and ensure fast access to most frequently used media. A world-wide Web client that facilities the multisearch capability and delivers ranked results. This system has an integrated frame-accurate VTR control of continuous media. IBM Digital Library provides a way for libraries and users to capture information and build them into new products quickly, whether it is today's broadcast, a new multimedia CD-ROM, magazine, or Internet product.

Some other important Digital Library Initiative projects and their site information.

1. The Networked Computer Science technical Reports Library a collection of computer Science technical reports from CS departments and industrial and government research laboratories.
2. The Networked Digital Library of Theses and Dissertations by pacing them online with the content in an accessible form, the works may be accessed through the Electronic Thesis and dissertation Library.
3. Library without Walls a broad based digital library project to make information available to researchers on their desktops on a network environment.
4. Thesaurus Linguarum Hiberni an interactive on-line searchable database archive of literary and historical materials in the various languages of early, mediaeval and modern Ireland.
5. Project Barley (Columbia University) a public library on the Internet.

6.15.5. MULTIMEDIA DATABASES

Now a days a large number of photographs, artifacts, audio recordings and textual material in various collections are available in libraries. Multimedia is helping the libraries in integrating all the information from various forms/sources subject-wise and making meaningful multimedia databases both for day-to day use archiving.

6.15.6 Multimedia Information Retrieval System

Hypermedia Information Retrieval System (HIRS) is hypertext version of large and comprehensive annotated bibliography of hypertext/hypermedia information. Compiled from a variety of sources including periodicals, academic journals and online informational databases, it is intended for educational and training purposes only and no warranty is made as to the suitability of anything included in this stack for any specific purposes.

6.15.7. Multimedia Catalogues

Interactive multimedia Catalogues are electronic forms of catalogues distributed in the mail-order catalogue market. Printed catalogues are one of the important information sources particularly in technical libraries. These catalogues consume large percentage of postal carrier bags. Today, the interactive multimedia catalogues offer a high volume of information on a small disk. Several international publishing companies are also bringing out their catalogues in interactive multimedia CD-ROMs for e.g. Catalogues, Macromedia Showcase, etc.

6.15.8. Multimedia Information Resources

The kinds of multimedia systems/information resources available in libraries and information centers include: (i) CD-ROMs: (ii) video discs(VD); (iii) laser discs(LD); (iv) audio & videocassettes; (v) web; (vi) databases on services; and (vii) digital video.

Many gib publishers have now converted their reference books including, encyclopedias, dictionaries, handbooks, etc from the traditional print form to multimedia format". Thus libraries have a choice of selecting either of the multimedia publications are listed below:

1. **Encyclopedias: Crompton's Interactive Encyclopedia, 1998** : Britannica CD 98 and Britannica Video CD; Encyclopedia, 1998 World Book Multimedia Encyclopedia; Microsoft Encarta 98 etc.
2. **Dictionaries and Directors** : Oxford English Dictionary; Webster English Dictionary; National Geographic's Mammals; British Birds; Microsoft Dinosaurs, etc.
3. **Reference Manuals** : MIT Movie Manual; Interactive Graphics Documents; The Manual of Medical therapeutics, etc.
4. **Year Books** : The Guniess Disk of records.
5. **Reference Books** : Earth quest; world Climate Disc; Interactive periodic Table, etc.
6. **Electronic Books** : Manual of Medical Therapeutics; The Electronic whole Earth Catalogue; Microsoft Musical Instruments; Introduction to Classical Music; The oxford Textbook of Medicine on CD-ROM, etc.

7. **Electronic Newspapers Journals** : The Times/ Sunday Tames/The Guardian Times, Newsweek; Multimedia Tech for Electronic Newspapers; Integrated Multimedia Environment; Music and Multimedia Publishing; ST and Medical Publishing for Electronic Delivery, etc.
8. **Multimedia Fiction** : Now a day several Multimedia fiction books/packages are available for all levels of people, for example. The manhole, a children fiction takes the kids to a fantasy world with talking animals and dragons where magic bean stalks grow into the sky.

6.15.9. Geographical Information Systems (GIS)

Additional multimedia information, visuals, audio and video can be associated along with landmarks and other points of interest in a Geographic information Systems. For example, In India, Bangalore. Online, is a multimedia GIS for several cities in India Number of commercial GIS reference tools are available in the market for libraries for their ready reference. These tools include: quick reference Atlas.

6.15.10. Electronic Publishing

The emergence of CD-writers and recordable CDs has solved some of the problems of the libraries in storing/archiving their less used materials. Multimedia tools along with CD-writers made possible in publishing information from different sources in a most easy to use and acceptable form to the library uses. Now several big libraries started publishing their special collections, image databases, OPACs, etc on multimedia CD-ROMs. It is one of the most viable alternatives to paper-based publishing.

6.15.11. Multimedia Archival System

Multimedia archival System are mostly developed by the national museums, publishing houses, movie production companies, etc" The Design Museum located in Butler's Wharf in London has stored information regarding 250 artifacts, 40 designers, 25 manufactures and 11 monuments on Mac using HyperCard. The museum of London has over 3 million archaeological files on 7-gigabyte storage space. Similarly ABC News has a very large size Macbased Video archival library for developing hypermedia applications. Project Jukebox is another HyperCard-based multimedia archival system for archiving multimedia information resources in the library.

6.15.12. Multimedia use in Museum Libraries

Multimedia systems allow images, sounds and text to be combined in imaginative new ways to be transmitted in digital formats and be stored and reproduced or networked for wide public access and use. to accelerate the Multimedia digitization of collections, to ensure their accessibility to the public and to stress its value as a learning resources for schools and universities. Global co-operation will help museums and galleries to increase public interest in their resources for the benefit of further enrichment the target users will be students, teachers, researchers, general public as well as curators and the endusers of the multimedia services provided by museums and Indian libraries are already using multimedia in their libraries for providing information services to their users and interactive museum displays.

6.15.13. Call Number Directories

A Call Number Directory program was using Macintosh's HyperCard at the Science and Engineering Library. The Science and Engineering Library houses materials pertaining to the life and physical sciences, computing, mathematics, and nurshing on seven floors. This programme helps the users in locating the information and also the physical locations of the books in different floors showing the pictures of those floors, stacks, etc. [23.24,25,26,27].

6.16. MULTIMEDIA PUBLISHING

Multimedia in the integration of several media for presentation. M-publishing includes ordering, correlating representations, organizing (layout, order) hypermedia linking, adding interactive scripts. It users the computer to integrate and control diverse electronic media such as computer screens, video displays, CD-ROM and speech and audio synthesizer. Further information distribution and using includes network distribution, optical publishing, online use, hypermedia enhancement by users. In the different MM publishing are shown in table 14.

Table 14. Multimedia Publishing

Medium	Collecting	Preparing
Vedio	Vedio edit list	Digitize, enhance, compress
Image	Selection	Digitize, enhance, compress
Audio	Audio edit list	Filter, degitize, enhance compress
Text	Text Filling	Text processing, too use
Graphics	(Composite) Object selection	Readering, drawing, animating tool use

MM technology allows all types all types of information includes full nation video, still images, audio, text and graphics to be stored and distributed on all digital source.

6.16.1. System Requirements

The standard PC systems do not have the necessary built-in hardware and software to handle audio and video information. So one needs MM PC shortly known as MPC.

The MPC can be any PC-AT/386 system or higher configuration fitted with a stereo audio card and CD-ROM drive of specified capabilities. A typical MM system will consist of a powerful workstation preferably 486 and above and for more common applications, an RISC workstation with minimum of 4 to 8 MB of main memory, over 100 MB of hard disc, a high quality of SVGA, colour monitor windows environment, mouse and the add on cards like sound blaster and vedio blaster card with the necessary software.

The different class of mm system is shown in table. These are different classes of MM system 100. These are

- First generation MMS
- Second generation MMS
- Third Generation MMS [28]

Table 15. Classes of Multimedia System

Components	*Multimedia*	*Typical current system*	*Typical advanced system*
Storage	CD-ROM 30 MB	CD-ROM, 100 MB CD-ROM gaga bites	
Processor	80286	80386 or MC 68030	80486 or MC 68040
Display	VGA	768 X 480	1.024 X 768
Extra board	Audio board	Next dimension CD-ROM XA, DVI	MPEG System

Networking	None	Ethernet, tokenring	Fiber distributed interface
Software	Windows 2.0	Multimedia Mediascript Media view	Integrator

6.16.2. Using the multimedia library to store media files

Before students can launch a multimedia file, you must store on a web server, in a Web Tools database, in the Learning Space Web Library, or attached to a Media Center document. After storing the file, you must tell the Media Center document where to go to retrieve the file. Learning Space uses and HTML tag called Passthru HTML for this retrieval process. Passthru HTML tags allow you to use HTML in your document to reference the media files and integrate them into the Media Helper takes you through the steps for adding passthru HTML to your Media Center document. Note : Notes users will only see the Passthru HTML tag.

To add media to the Learning Space Web Library

* From within the Media Center, click the Create New Entry button. 

* Click the Media Helper action button. 

* Select **Web Users** and click ok.

* Select "Go to the Multimedia Library" and click OK.

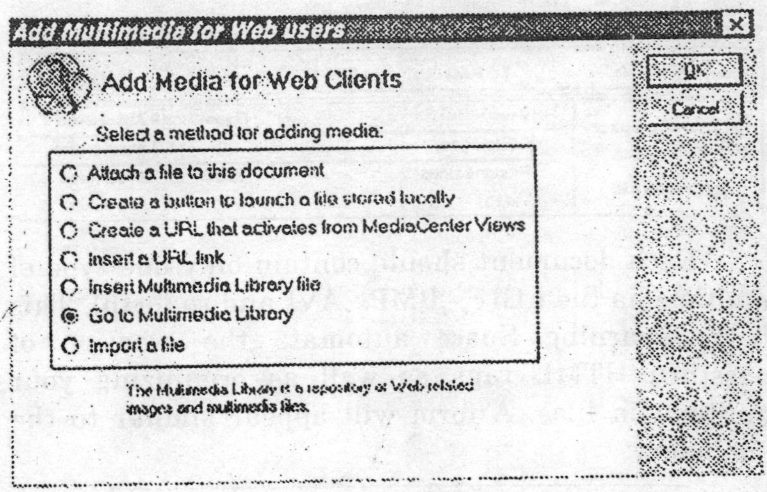

* The following dialog box will appear. Simply click the OK button to continue.

* Click on the New Media Doc button to create a new container (containers are like categories, for example, Education GIF Images might be a container that includes all the GIF Images used in Education Learning Space courses).

* Or Select an existing container where you want to add a new file by clicking on a container title from the list provided and click on the Edit Media Doc button.

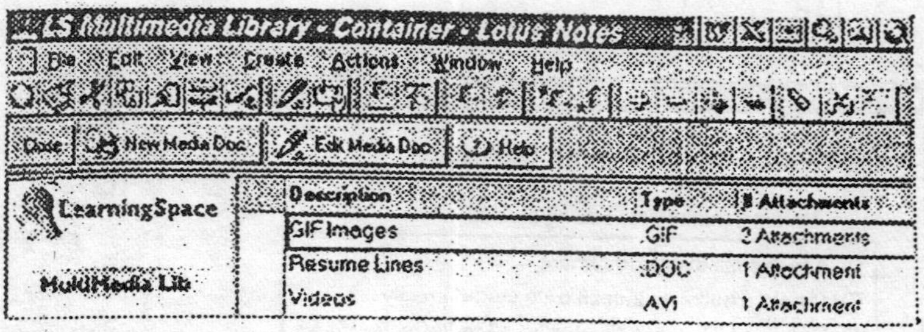

Each document should contain only one type of multimedia file (.GIF, .BMP, .AVI and so forth). This helps Learning Space automate the creation of passthru HTML tags as well as organizing your multimedia files. A form will appear similar to the one below.

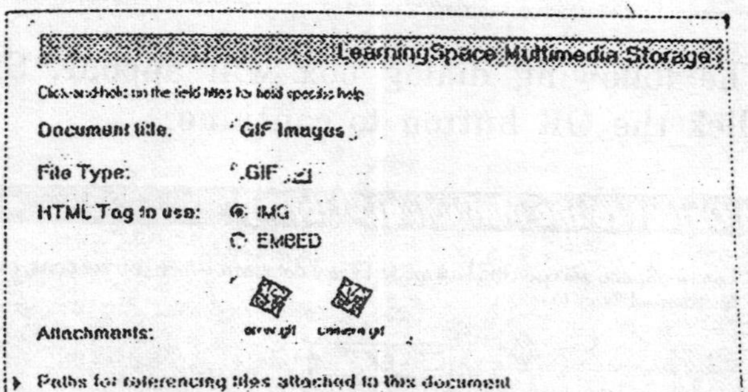

* In the Document Title field, enter a title to identify the contents of the container document.
* In the File type field, enter the three-letter extension of the files you will be storing in the container document. To select from a list of file extensions, click the arrow next to the field. You will see a dialog box like the one below. Click on the extension that you want and click OK. If you don't see the extension you want, type a new extension in the New Keywords area and click OK.

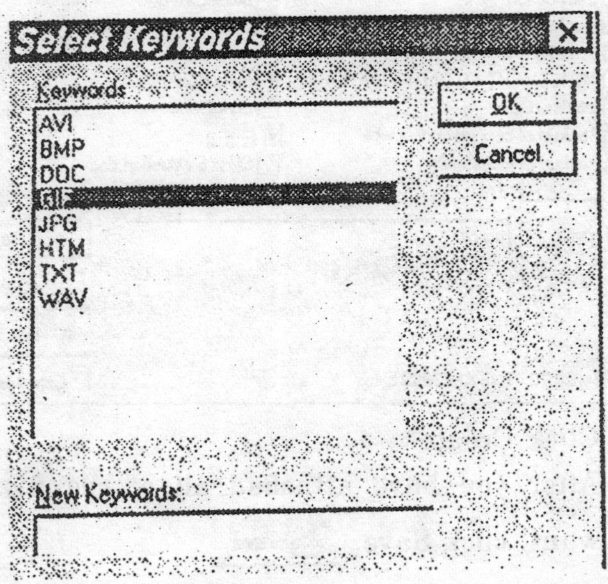

* In the HTML Tag to Use field, select IMG or EMBED. Make sure you choose the appropriate HTML tag type. If neither type is appropriate, make no selection.

IMG tag - loads a referenced image file into a document. (.GIF, .BMP, .JEPG)

EMBED tag · loads a referenced multimedia file into a document and initializes the player associated with it. (.AVI, Animated GIF, .WAV).

* Click the Attach Files button. 

* Select the file you want to store in the container from the Create Attachments dialog box as shown below.

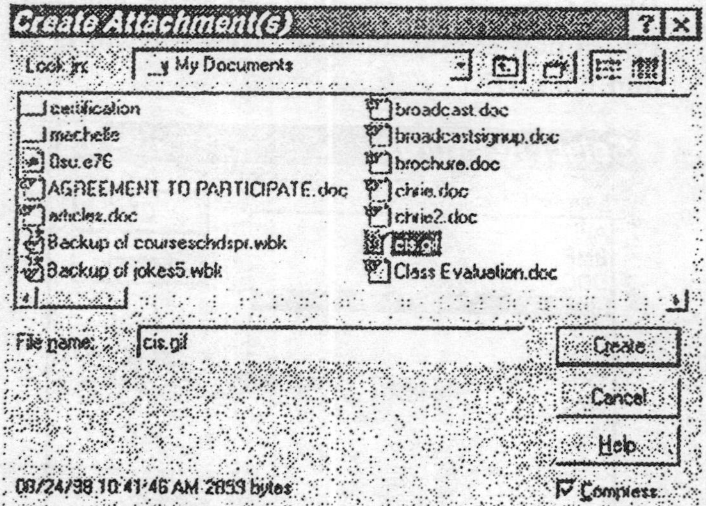

* Click Create.
* After you have attached all of the files you want, click Save. 

* Click Close to close the Learning Space Multimedia Library.[29,30] 

6.16.2. Multimedia Layer model to user

MM is a set of new technology for the capture, manipulation, presentation and integration of various types of data, including audio, image, motion, video, animation, graphics and text. The original data can be in either analogue or digital form. Different layers of MM are shown in table 16.

Table 16. Different layers of Multimedia

Layer	*Description/contents*
Application	Hypertext, hypermedia, interactive Multimedia
Presentation	Devices: Keyboard, Mouse, Speakers, windows
	Media: animations, audio, graphics, images
	Vedio: operations: accessing, editing, sequencing, transforming
Session	History management, user induction, versioning
Base	Searching and interfacing with data, information and
	knowledge bases
View	Frames, graphs. lists, relations
Link	Labels, link identifiers types.
Node	Basic & composite media objects indentifiers
Communication	File systems, messages, processes

6.16.4. Standards for Multimedia

Initially, standards for digital MM were established by facet Recently, important new international standard for images audio and video have been accepted by electronics. Computer and communication organizations through consensus with the standards groups: Table present the summery of standards for MM.

Table 17. Standards for Multimedia

Short name	*Standard Group*	*Purpose*
JPEG	Joint photographic expert group	Digital compression & coding of continuous still images
H.261	Specialist group on coding for Visual telephony	Vedio coder/decoder for audio visual services.
MPEG	Moving picture expert group	Coding of moving pictures associated audio
MHEG	Multimedia & Hypermedia Interaction coding expert group	Coded representation of MM & HM information.
HYTime	Standard Music representation work Group.	HM/Time-based Strictiromg language

6.16.5. Multimedia Workstation

A multimedia workstation equipped with integrated computer, laserdisc player, CD-ROM drive, sound card, and VCR is available. Software available includes Win/TV, PODIUM, PowerPoint, Corel PhotoPaint, and Astound. Users are able to capture and download images and sounds from videos, CD-ROMs, and videodiscs in the library collection for use in presentations. The station is also connected to cable and the Internet, providing access to almost limitless visual resources[3].

6.17. SOFTWARE FOR EVERYONE

Most of the multimedia titles produced today are designed for home use. These titles fall into three broad categories: reference, which brings the resources of the public library into the home; education, which supplements classroom schooling; and entertainment. Within each category, certain genres have been established: the cartoon adventure and the interactive movie A four category, services covers wider multimedia applications in workplaces, public galleries, shopping malls, and even air plains.

6.17.1. Multimedia in Business

The application, which include in business are marketing, advertising, presentations, training, product demonstrations, databases catalogue, network communications, voice mail conference (conference is provide through local area network and wide area network).

Multimedia in training has become common. The manager can describe the process of making their product, used in making the budging and identity card databases. A new generation of interactive television and networked multimedia online business to business is evolving. These services delivered through interactive television and networked multimedia. These cases are much easier to construct, have short payback periods and require less investment than residential services proposal.

6.17.2. Multimedia at Homes

Television/VCR are platform for multimedia project at home, because currently television enjoys much higher penetration than home computers. The multimedia viewed on these sets will likely arrive on a pay and use basis. However computer with an attached CD-ROM drive cebome platform because of

- Present users/people are becoming familiar with computer.
- Marketing of homes computers reach saturation point.
- Game software developers are not the least.
- The incremental cost of adding CD-ROM drive and sound board to a home computer is now almost marginal.

6.17.3. Multimedia in Schools/Colleges

Multimedia made the great changes in the traditional teaching methods. In coming days teachers are become guide or supervisors. In laboratory the students can do experiments themselves through multimedia. The teacher becomes supervisor to explain the process.

6.17.4. Multimedia in Public Places

Multimedia provides information and help to

the people/tourist in hotels, railway station, bus station, shopping complex, museums etc. This installation may replace to traditional information booths and personnel: The user/people can work around the clock whenever he wants information/ help.

6.17.5. Multimedia in Sports

Multimedia plays a dominant role in training the sportsman. Through this we can train the sports man from traditional methods. The wrester can learn how to use the techniques in the matches. He can see the great matches through which he can understand what are precautions to be taken. The training may give through slides or transparency.

6.17.6. Multimedia for Entertainment

We can use multimedia as the radio/tape recorder to listen the news, song; it can be used as a newspaper to know the current awareness (through Internet) it can be used as a television for entertainment. Through this we can see the game and we can also play the game. Carton films can also be viewed.

6.17.7. Multimedia in Library

Present multimedia applications can be categorized into computer aided learning and computer base training. Through computer - aided learning the use may known the when the doors of information's are opened. What are the information sources available, what are the information services provide to the user. How to use the catalogue in searching the information which system issued classify the documents in library and which are the rules and regulations to be followed. And other things can be known thorough computer aided learning. Without going to the library we can see how the library is i.e. its building, sources, services through multimedia.

6.17.8. Multimedia at work

Outside the home, multimedia is taking on new and varied roles. In businesses, CD-ROMs new used to train the products in museums and public places information booths act as local guides. And in skies, multimedia is transforming the concepts of in the fight services.

6.18. ONE-SUBJECT ENCYCLOPEDIAS

General encyclopedias have long been a multimedia standard, but now an increasing number of titles cover just one subject everything form is represented. Single-subject encyclopedia have two advantages ove the general sort: first, being narrower in scope, they can go into much more detail and second, they office present information in a more interesting way. The way a title presents information, its "look and feel", is known as its interface. General encyclopedias include so many different types of information that they have to use all-purpose interfaces, which are often fairly bland. One-subject titles, however can build information into a graphical world specially created to entice the user into it.

6.19. INFORMATION CENTER

The main screen of the encyclopedia of Nature is a naturalist's console, complete with spinning globe, desk drawers, barometer, reference books and other artifacts. This acts as a pictorial contents page-every object represents a different subject area.

The graphical interface encourages exploration and offers many ways into the encyclopedia's body of information.

6.20. LEISURE PURSUITS

Leisure titles are among the fastest expanding multimedia sales areas. Books for the hobbyist and the enthusiast have always comprised a large part of publishing, and this storage market is being tapped for its multimedia potential. Books can offer a great deal, but more through the range of information they cover on any one subject than through flexibility and presentation, and it is precisely in this area of presentation that multimedia has the advantages.

6.21. INTERACTIVE MUSEUMS

Visiting a modern museum or art gallery is perhaps the original multimedia experience a combination of many of the elements that have made CD-ROM based multimedia so successful. The exhibits in a museum are accompanied by written information. Visual displays, and sometimes video presentations, and you can listen to expert commentary from a tour guide or on cassette. In addition, the exhibits are so arranged that you can browse through them and explore the information in your own way. Becaise museums so successfully combine various media in this way, they have given multimedia producers a useful model on which to base one-subject encyclopedia titles.

6.22. THE WORLD OF MULTIMEDIA

Multimedia software arrived in the mid-eighties, in the form of the CD-ROM. By the early nineties, the multimedia phenomenon was gathering momentum and had attracted great journalistic interest. The invention of the CD-ROM. With its capacity to store vast amounts of information, was being compared in significance to the invention of paper, the printing press, and photography. Even if multimedia does not live up to the hype, it is already a multimedia-dollar industry. Over 300 new CD-ROM titles make their way onto the shelves of computer and bookstores every month. And many of them put computers to uses that could not possibly have been anticipated when multimedia first took off.

6.22.1. Browse the world

One of the most common reference common reference books is the home is the atlas. Multimedia atlas presents the same information in a more dynamic and involving way. Navigating around the world is made easy and every country is brought to life with multimedia features such as sound animations, satellite and time-lapse photography, and video clips with a good multimedia atlas you search for a place name and find yourself at its map locations in seconds.

6.22.2. Multimedia Atlases

Like the book atlas, the multimedia version contains maps, illustrations, tables and statistical data relating to the whole world, as we well as to regions and countries. Multimedia's unique twist is that it uses sound, video and animation to present this information more vividly. It also allows the user to make a large number of choices about the way each map is displayed.

6.22.2.1. Control the World

With many titles, you can decide how much

detail and what kind of details you want to see on screen. The scale of maps can be adjusted using zoom bottoms. You can also choose the features that appear on the maps, or you can add new locations. Most multimedia titles contain large databases of statistical information.

6.22.2.2. Using the 3D atlas

The main screen of Multimedia Corporation's 3D atlas features a globe and a find box. You can rotate the three-dimensional globe about any axis and zoom in to see individual countries or regions in more detail. You can also specify the type or amount of details to be displayed. In addition, you can mark places that are significant to you with map pins and include text and pictures that you can view whenever you come back to the location in future.

6.23. THE MULTIMEDIA MAGAZINE

It could be many years before daily or even weekly news can be supplied in an interactive form on CD-ROMs, but multimedia publishers have already begun producing several magazines. These multimedia magazines each arrive on a single CD-ROM every one or two months and present their information via a graphical interface, using the full range of multimedia techniques. They offer the reader a completely new to interact with a magazines contains.

6.23.1. Newsweek Interactive

Claiming to be the worlds first interactive news magazine, Newsweek Interactive combines an archive of three months worth of Newsweek with four hours of radio interviews from the weekly program" Newsweek on Air". Each edition also contains two large feature articles, which combine the journalistic and analytical expertise of the Newsweek team with multimedia and hypertext elements [32.33].

6.24. MULTIMEDIA EDUCATION

Traditionally, a major goal of universities has been to equip students with an intellectual culture that enables them to adapt to changing work environments for the duration of their careers. This is achieved by instilling in students more than just knowledge of facts or tol skills. Students need the mental apparatus required for them to self-learn new skills, and more importantly, understand and are able to deploy new technologies in their fields as they arise. A university course should strive to achieve this is order to provide long-term benefits for the students themselves and society as a whole. As important as preparing graduates for careers in multimedia, the other principal goal of undergraduate studies and supply potential researchers in the field. This requires that students have a profound understanding of the principles and theoretical constructs underlying multimedia systems. The first researchers in multimedia were electrical engineers, followed by researchers in IT, and then from education and psychology. Clearly, most of the current research in multimedia requires a solid background in one of these disciplines.

Ultimately, academics need to decide what is to be expected from their graduates. These expectations will determine the constraints, directions, and standards that identify the course. This presents the first major hurdle in developing a curriculum for multimedia and can be restated as a rather contentious question: What is multimedia? In multimedia solely multimedia information, that is, mainly concerned with the process of its creation or authoring? If the answer is "yes", then multimedia is relegated to being predominantly just another creative arts genre, and most definitively not a computing discipline. In other words, is multimedia the message or the medium, or a combination of both?

That multimedia presents a new paradigm in information handling and delivery, with intrinsic support for profound interaction, is indisputable. This interactivity cannot be isolated from the medium for it is the very medium itself-the digital computer-which mediates its provision. While in some respects the multimedia revolution is akin to the dawn of television, in others it is radically different. Television is a multimedia broadcast technology primarily for experiencing events displaced in space and time that could equally be experienced without the technology by being present in person at the event. In television, the message and the medium are traditionally independent of each other. In contrast, multimedia cannot be experienced without the technology because it is the technology that creates the experience. Multimedia is not just another genre; it is a fusion of both the medium and the message to conceive interactive, multimedia information spaces effectively in the form of an artificial environment. These constantly evolving environments are created by a combination of computer processing and interface hardware, software programs and at least two or more digital modalities of data. The fact remains that many multimedia systems such as hospital information systems will never contain authored content. An education in multimedia should empower students to be proficient in creating these artificial interactive, multimedia environments and not just content authoring using certain software packages.

The very nature of these environments is highly fluid and under constant evolution. These may be distributed or centralized systems involving either synchronous or a synchronous communication. They may be fully impressive or handheld, law-band-width wireless systems. They may have stringent security requirements or utilize visual, acoustic, or haptic interfaces. Hence, if multimedia is to be considered an emerging new specialist discipline, it must, while borrowing heavily from other disciplines, focus on integrating certain elements from these to create application-specific, artificial, interactive, multimedia environments on any platform. This entails much more than just being skilled in the use of authoring packages, it requires a profound understand of the underlying host systems and technologies.

6.24.1. Careers and Vocational Training

To envision the multimedia industry as restricted to content authoring is like mistaking the scope of an iceberg by only considering the portion above water. Multimedia encompasses much more than that, but these activities are often under the guise of traditional vocations. Those developing interactive television, multiplayer video games, online film libraries, or hospital information systems are just as much involved in the multimedia industry as graphic designers are. Indeed, the majority of people working in multimedia have technical, not artistic, backgrounds. For a person with appropriate training, the scope of possible careers in multimedia is wide-ranging.

Multimedia practice tends to exhibit their main focal point; the authoring, application, or system levels. Training undergraduates to function at the authoring level requires much more than just training in the use of the tools. While workers need to know how to use their tools well, good workers need to understand the nature of the raw material they are working with, especially when it is rapidly evolving. This is a significant issue with multimedia.

Digital video up to and including the MPEG-2 standard has simply been a precomposited unstructured bit stream. With MPEG-4, digital video is defined as a structured set of unrendered objects to be composited and rendered at routine. The nature of multimedia data will continue to evolve with data models and representations becoming more abstract, and the interactions with and operations that may be performed on the data become increasingly varied and powerful. The implication of this is not just the rapid obsolescence of tools but also that the methods of working with the students have only been tool skilled without an understanding principles of multimedia data representations. He of the media data representations many will have difficulties in adapting to new tools and will not be able to exploit the full capabilities of the new systems.

Apart from data, the presentation environments for the data are also evolving. This is due to the use of specialized platforms for hosting multimedia such as set-top boxes for interactive television and band limited, low power mobile systems. Graduates in multimedia should be able to deal with these emerging environments. The type of content in multimedia systems is also evolving. Graduates must not be

Table 18. Multimedia career opportunities

Level	*Authoring*	*Application*	*System*
Email	Content Creation By using Authority tools	Creation of multimedia Software applications By using programming Tools	Creaction and running of entire multimedia systems by bringing together all components
Typical Example	Multimedia Education/ Training materials	Multimedia authoring Tools	Information systems Such as hospitals
	Online books/ Publications	Hypermedia viewers/browsers	Entertainment systems (games)
	Multimedia Advertising/ Business materials	Multimedia data editors	Business systems, Information kiosks, and so forth
	Creating 3D Animation and movie special effects	Multimedia database Management systems	Communication system Computer-mediated Collaborative work

limited to only creating aesthetically pleasing graphic designs; they must be able to handle content in multimedia databases or dynamic or intelligent agent in virtual environments. Aside from changing environments, tools, and data, effective content authoring many require knowledge in the more traditional areas of human factors, educational psychology, advertising principles, video producion, graphics, and sound design, to name a few fields.

Most multimedia authoring efforts are highly dependent on very technically skilled professionals. The main reason for this is that graphic designers in general do not have the necessary background and skills to quickly adapt to new technology and tools used for the high end work had to be developed in-house, consumer tools often being insufficient. For example, broadcast TV does not use the standard VCR-level video and users must know how to handle substantially more complex equipment and have a more fundamental understanding of video than as polarized fields on magnetic videotape.

If a multimedia degree course is only going to provide graduates with the skills to create content, then it is subscribing to the concept that multimedia is just another arts genre and therefore not part of a technology-based discipline. Multimedia authoring involves more than just creating new content; it also involves integrating existing content into a multimedia system. This often requires the development of database interfaces within the authoring environment to enable users to access stored data. This database access may need to support multiple query or browsing interfaces and provide advanced reporting functionality such as intelligent filtering of query results. The content may also consist of software simulations of financial, scientific or engineering systems for educational, entertainment, or business purposes. Integrating this existing content into a multimedia system requires additional software development skills.

In essence, any information space is characterized by three dimensions: its logical structure, its content, and its representation or layout and rendition of the content. In any multimedia information space, due to the complexity of the content and its representations the role of the logical structure is predominant to a large degree in determining the success of the system. Therefore, it is widely accepted that the main problem in multimedia is not the creation of new content, but the design of the information space so that the content is easy to access and present to reduce congestive overload and facilitate osmosis of the information. This involves deterministically designing the linkages, information structures, and state transitions to ensure that the architectural integrity of the information space is not compromised.

The application level involves the creation of multimedia software applications. This covers everything from applets to authoring tools, multimedia presentation engines, or multimedia database management systems. To function at the application level, graduates need to have a solid foundation in object-oriented software design, programming, human computer interaction, multimedia information management, and distributed systems. Graduates must also have a strong understanding of computer graphics, multimedia data compression algorithms, and data formats. They need to know how to perform lów-level manipulation of multimedia data and how to interface to a range of multimedia hardware and other software systems.

6.24.2. Multimedia Research

Multimedia research can be segregated into two main categories:

1. Research into multimedia systems. And,
2. Research that applies multimedia to classical endeavors.

Multimedia systems research is technological in nature and involves investigating multimedia data models, system architectures, information management, and compression and processing of multimedia data.

Research mainly focuses on assessing the assessing the impact of multimedia on their enterprises, as in assessing the impact of multimedia on education and decision support systems. The majority of multimedia research is traditionally of the first category. (Table 19) classifies some of the existing.

6.24.3. Curriculum Design

We have considered the skills and knowledge that may be expected from a potential multimedia degree graduate. We have seen that multimedia can only exit as a fusion of technologies, hardware, software and multimedia degree in multimodal data to form artificial environments. Hence, a degree in multimedia data in multimedia should equip students with proficiency in creating these interactive multimodal information spaces. To do this students must be provided with in-depth knowledge of both standalone and distributed multimedia computing system including the various interaction mechanisms.

Table 19 : Multimedia research areas

Type1	*Info. Management*	*Info Processing*	*Data Compression*	*Communication Systems*
	Content-based Retrieval	Expert Systems	Audio Coding	Multimedia service
	Hypermedia Systems	Recognition	Video Coding	Provision
	Resource discovery	Understanding	Image Coding	Mobile multimedia Systems
				Distrusted services
Type2	Education and Training	Psychology	Management	Data Visualization
	Instructional Design	Cognition	Decision Support	Data Signification
	Distance eduction		System simulation	Use of haptic interfaces

This also requires some expertise in software development and the preparation of mulrtmodal data. We should notice here that the preparation of the data constitutes about a quarter of the components of multimedia Indeed, a multimedia curriculum may be considered unbalanced if it is concerned with content creation to a greater proportion.

Multimedia is devices and rapidly evolving discipline. Much of the activity central of multimedia does not takes place under the umbrella of multimedia, but goes by the name of more traditional vocations. Training graduates to be proficient in developing multimedia systems and assuring the long-term value of this training requires clear discernment regarding the real nature of the multimedia phenomenon part from more classical endeavors.

6.25. MULTIMEDIA EDUCATIONAL TECHNOLOGY IN IMPARTING LIS EDUCATION

According to, a models curriculum in information studies prepared by J. A. Large under general information Programme and UNISIST, UNISCO. The Rapid Rate of technological development in information storage, retrieval and transmission, necessities the storage technological emphasis of information studies." The Thirteenth Annual convention and conference of the society. For information Science was held in New Delhi during 27-29 January 1994, with the theme "perspectives of Multimedia information service in India". The following recommendations emerged form the discussions at the four technical sessions:

1. In view of its complexity and time bound nature information management is bound to play a

major role in different sections of the society.

2. To keep pace with the world developments and fast changing technologies, there is a need to involve NGO's private sectors and other voluntary organizations in a coordinated way.
3. In order to optimize the use of multimedia in information management there is a need to bring all the allied organizations connected with informatics under one umbrella and consider holding of an Indian information congress.

Library and Information Science (LIS) education is a professional education and it is a specialized area of human training. Preparation of Librariaship and information work requires a mastery of the body of knowledge and techniques utilized in library and information operations, and services, which constitute. The discipline 'Library and Information Science'. The primary aim of education for library and information Science should be the training of the intellect in matters pertaining to human knowledge and information, and goal should be the achievement of the highest wisdom in promoting to human knowledge and information, and its goal should be the achievement of the heist wisdom is promoting the utilization of knowledge and information for the benefit man kind.

Till recently the LIS curriculum in the country was concerned mainly with the professional techniques used in the organization of resources. However, the changing information environment has a great input on production of manpower though LIS education. Education that responds only to today's needs fails to provide tomorrow's learners.

Hence, it is evidence that the LIS student ought to gain expertise in the acquisition and use of LIS education to introduce a paper on 'Multimedia Technology' either as core or optical paper depending on the load of the curriculum.

So far as media is concerned, the information may be stored on multimedia, viz., and magnetic tape. Electronic, optical desks, video films, videodisc, microfilms, photographic films, etc. A combination of theoretical teaching with actual situation encompassing all the aspects in this area is imperative in a dynamic curriculum. Further more, new changes of modern technology forecast a paper less society. The basic need is to against new librarians with selection process methods. Conservation and preservation, application in conservation and management of multimedia resources. It is a new era of information service, requiring new set of media selection skills to handle them [34,35,36].

2.26. MULTIMEDIA PRESENTATION

There are many tools or software's for designing a multimedia presentation available in the market. These can be categorized into mainly 3 kinds of software: presentation packages hypermedia programs and authoring systems, there is an overlap among these classifications. For example some presentation packages provide a limited hypermedia capability while hypermedia programs can create simple presentations and full-fledged authoring systems can do just about anything. Hence, depending upon requirements, one can select appropriate package.

Presentation Packages product-convincing multimedia shows consisting of slides, audio clips, animations and full-monom sequences based on linear slide-show metaphor. Several graphics packages also have presentation capacities. Example: Powerpoint, Harvard Graphics and so on.

2.26.1. Power Point

Power point is software that provides a complete environment for authoring, drawing, pack aging, formatting, and charting and many input/output tasks.

Based on the slide-show metaphor (automatic/ manual slide-show feature), Power point has a slide sorter that sets us to drag slides and position them in the order we want to present them. We can separately create, edit and arrange each slide.

Power point has a clip art library of more than 1,100 business graphics, a graphing feature to create customized figures, an organization chart creator, and an equation editor to create and display scientific and mathematic equations.

We can drag and drop slides, graphics, data from one presentation or application another, and we can embed images, slides and presentation from Power Point into other applications. Importing charts and spreadsheet data from Microsoft Excel as well as building live links between Power point and other applications are also possible. An AutoContent wizard" helps us to figure out what to say, and an Outliner helps organize and recorder thoughts by letting us to selectively collapse and expand outline headings.

2.26.2. Harvard Graphics

Harvard Graphics is a high-powered graphics package with presentation capabilities, published by

Software Publishing Corporation. There are 31 professionally designed presentation styles, where each style specifics the charting options, color palette, background design and type font for a presentation. Appearance of every slide can be changed automatically by editing a presentation's master template. A chart gallery contains preformatted title bullet, table, data and organizational carts.

Harvard Graphics lets us add special efforts to text or drawings and multimedia capacities allow adding music, video and animation. Its print options enables to create speaker notes, handouts, transparencies and slides on laser printer, plotter, color printer or film recorder. Like Power point Harvard Graphics has OLE (Object Linking and Embedding) supports that lets network users display presentations on up to 64 other computers simultaneously. Presentation can be viewed in outline format with the Outliner, or as a slide show in the Slide Sorter. The Quick-Looks feature allows us to try different colors, fonts and perspectives to see how slides look before committing any change.

6.26.3. Hypermedia Programs

Hypermedia Programs provide an infinite capability to link objects and enable users to negative among them. Example Tool book, podium, etc.

6.26.3.1. Tool Book

Tool book is published by asymmetric (country). Its purpose is to reduce the amount of time and effort required creating Windows applications. Multimedia applications can be developed by creating books full of pages, which can contain text, graphics and buttons that enable user interaction.

Tool book has a scripting language called Open Script, in which handlers can be written. Handlers are code modules that define the response to any event that occurs in the application. Events may be user interaction, navigation and so on. Tool book comes with more than 270 prescripted multimedia objects called widgets, which can be copied and pasted to any new applications.

6.26.3.2.1. Podium

Podium is a hypermedia product invented at the University of Delaware in 1988. It gives multimedia toolbox, which makes it quick and easy to create multimedia applications.

6.26.4. Authoring systems

An authorizing is a set of full - fledged application development tools that allows us to present material, ask questions about it, evaluate user input and branch accordingly in a multimedia presentation.

6.26.4.1. Macromedia Author ware Interactive Studio

Author ware is the most powerful autoring environment for creating interactive presentations. An advantage authorware has over most other packages is that it can be used to create applications for both Windows and Macintosh users. it features major advancements in ease of use, tools integration, productivity, extensibility, Internet and Intranet delivery and database connectivity. It gives non-programmers the power to create, deliver and maintain interactive applications.

The author was creates an application by selection icons and dragging them onto the flow line. By double-clicking an icon opens it, allowing the author to add content. As icons accumulate on the screen, the author can click the Map icon to group related icons together. Thus, the author can view the application from a top-down approach, maintaining perspective on how the various program modules interrelate.

6.26.4.2. Icon Author

In Icron Author, an application structure is built by dragging icon form an icon palette into a flowchart that depicts the logic of the application. Then each icon is opened to reveal a dialog box that allows the properties and the content of that object to be defined. No scripting is required and there is no language. There are about 50 types of icons, which provide support for nearly all computer functions and all multimedia functions.

6.26.5. Steps in creating multimedia presentation

Creating an interactive multimedia presentation is like making a feature film. A typical multimedia presentation may involve the following major steps.

6.26.5.1. Concepts

The objectives for the project are defined, and the type of application is specified. In the movies, this is the stage at which the producer decides what kind of movie he wants to make and what the subject will be.

6.26.5.2. Design

This is the process of deciding in detail what will be the project (what the content material is) and how it will be presented. In the movies, this would include script writing, casting and scene design steps.

6.26.5.3. Collecting content material

During this stage all the data audio and images, for the project are collected in appropriate digital formats. In the movies, this would be the production stage, where all the scenes for the movie are set up one by one and shot on film.

6.26.5.4. Assembly

In this step, the overall structure of the project is built, presentations are built in. In the movies, this is the postproduction-editing step, although it is the much simpler because there is no interactivity in a movie. A tool for this stage of authoring is called an assembly program.

6.26.5.5. Testing

During testing, the application is run and checked to confirm that it does exactly what the author intended. In the movies, this is similar to screening, where the movie or parts of it are viewed and approved by management people.

6.26.5.6. Distribution

In this step, the application is reproduction and delivered to end users for their use. In the movies, this movies, this would be the release and sistribution phase.

6.26.6. Preparing the presentation

6.26.6.1. Organizational Chart

One of the important steps in this project was

to develop and organizational chart. This chart helped in identifying the topics to be covered in the presentation. (Fig. 15).

6.26.6.2. Script Writing

Based on the organizational chart, the presentation script was developed. The main areas covered in this presentation are as follows:

1. Introduction
2. Organizational structure
3. Resources
4. Information Services
5. Publicity and User Orientation
6. Training Program
7. R&D and Consultancy Projects
8. Publications
9. Awards and Honours
10. Workshops and Seminars.

6.26.6.3. Slides Preparation:

Slides are prepared depending upon the script. PowerPoint provides an AutoContent Wizard, which guides us while creating a new presentation. Each slide can be separately created or edited. Slides can also be arranged or recordered as and when required.

6.26.6.4. Audio recording

One of the important steps in any multimedia presentation is audiorecording while recording audio care should be taken to fitter out external noise.

This step involves recording the voice for the commentary and selecting music to synchronize with the presentation.

6.26.6.5. Assembling

Once the slides and audio files are ready, the next step is to integrate them, i.e.. mixing or combining the appropriate audio files with the respective slides [37,38].

Multimedia will be one of the important information technologies. It is very effective presentation tool or system as compared to an ordinary textual presentation for communication of information. It satisfies the user in all aspects and especially interactive multimedia makes user to choose any sequence to view the information.

REFERENCES

1. SETH, M.K., Multimedia Librarianship in 2000 A.D. *International Library Movement*. Vol.
2. KJELLDAJHL, L, ed., Multimedia: systems interaction and application. : 1st *Eurographic workshop*, April 18-19, Berlin : Springer Verlag, 1991.
3. PATEL, C and RUSSEL, D., Multimedia concept in TV production unit and its usefulness. *20th IASLIC Conference*, 26-29 December, Lucknow, 1995.
4. SINGH, S.N. and GARG B.S., Role of multimedia/ Hypermedia in biological information services in India. *Annals of Library Science and Documentation* 42(1)m 1995, PP 1-17.
5. MARTIN, G: Multimedia: Technology looking for an application, *ASLIB*, 20(4), 1992.
6. FIEDMAN, TONY., Multimedia, New York: BluePrint, 1993. PP 1-20.
7. Ibid.,
8. BIRADAR, B.S. and KUMBAR, M., Role of multimedia hypermedia hypertext in the present information environment. **In :** SATYANARAYANA, B eds., *Multimedia its applications in library and information science*, Chennai, T.R, 1998. PP 161-165.

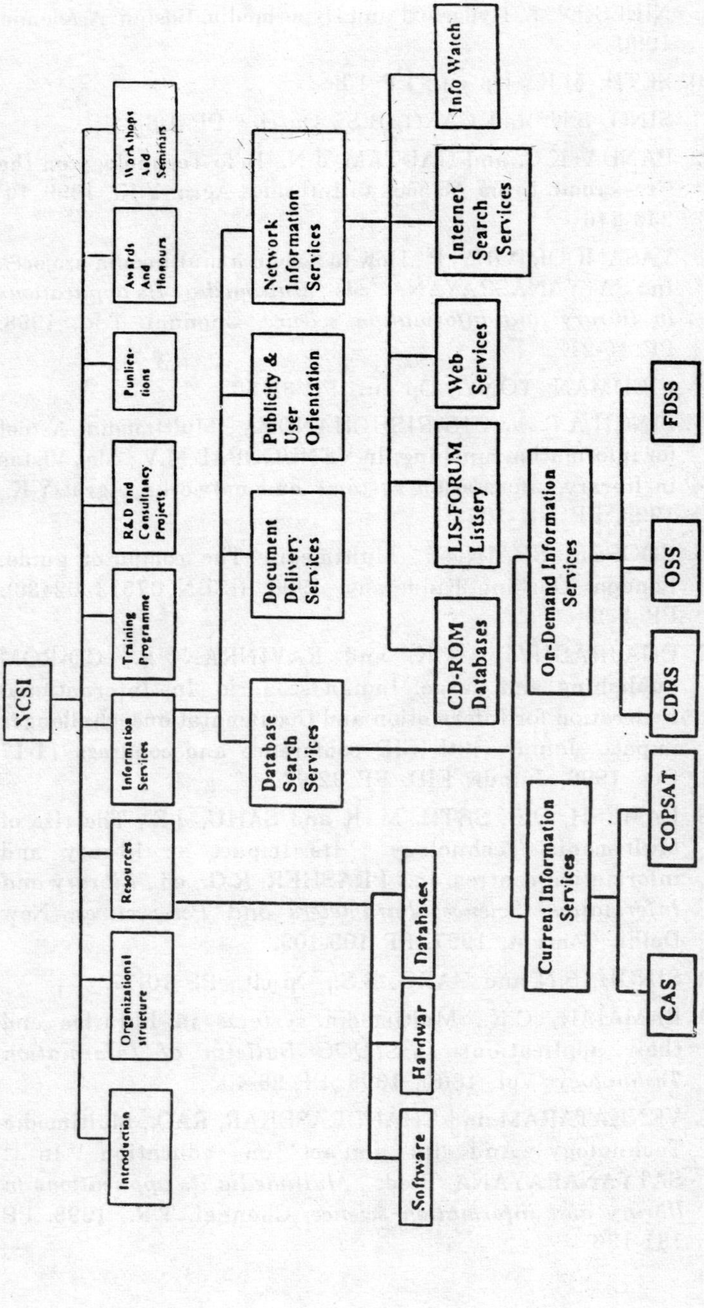

Fig. 15. NCSI functional Organizational Chart

9. NIELSON, J., Hypertext and Hypermedia, Boston: Academic, 1990.

10. SETH, M.K., Op cit., PP 1-8.

11. SING, S.N. and GARG, B.S., Op cit., PP 1-8.

12. PANDA, K.C. and GAUTAM, J.N., In'fo Technology on the Cross'road: From Ab'acus to Internet. Agra: Y.K., 1999. PP 230-246

13. VASAMOORTGHY, P., How to design a multimedia project?. In : SATYANASRAYANA., eds., *Multimedia : Its applications in library and information science*, Chennai: T.R., 1998. PP 15-21.

14. FIEDMAN, TONY., Op cit., PP 35-50.

15. SINGH,A.P. and HARISHCHANDRA., Multimedia: A tool for information mapping. In:VENUGOPAL,M.V., eds., Vistas in library information systems and networks, Agra: Y.K., 1999. PP 101-106.

16. COOPER, BRAIN ed., Multimedia: The computer guide, London: Dorking Kindershy, 1996. (ISBN 07513 02430). PP 1-30

17. CGAJRABIRTY, A.K. and RAVINRAN, S., CD-ROM publishing and usage: Indian scenario. In: International Federation for Information and Documentations, challenges impact, Jaipur: 49th FID conference and congress 11-17 Oct. 1998, Jaipur: FID, PP 92-97.

18. RAMESH, D.B. SETH, M. K and SAHU, J.R., The rise of Multimedia Technology : Its impact on library and information centres. In : PRASHER, R.G., ed., *Library and Information Science: Parameters and Perspectives*, New Delhi: Concept, 1997. PP 105-109.

19. SINGH, S.N and GARG, B.S., Op cit., PP 10-17.

20. RAMAIAH, C.K., Multimedia systems in libraries and their applications *DESIDOC Bulletin of Information Technology*. Vol. 18(6), 1998. PP 28-40.

21. VENKATARAM and CHANDRASEKAR, RAO., Multimedia Technology And its impact on education. In : SATYANARAYANA, B eds., *Multimedia its applications in library and information science*, Chennai. T.R., 1998. PP 131-136.

22. SINGH, J and KAUR, N., Digital multimedia: Impact on society technological developments and applications. In : ASSOCIATION OF INDIAN UNIVERSITIES., *Information technologies on higher education*, New Delhi : AIU, 2000. PP 41-50.

23. RAMAIAH, C.K. Op cit. PP 28-40.

24. KUMBAR, MALLINATH and BIRADAR, B.S., Multimedia Technology and its impact on education. In : RAJU, A.A.A and Others, eds., *Information Technology and Its impact on LIS education and management*, Delhi : DELTA, 1997. PP 97-105.

25. AMUDAVALLI, A., Multimedia and its application. In : SATYANARAYANA, B eds., ***Multimedia its applications in library and information science***, Chennai, T.R., 1998. PP 205.

7

Multimedia Networking

So networking of computer based multimedia is possible. However network delivery of multimedia is not new, the broadcast television system has been available since the 1950's. The difference now is that the information which has previously been presented on radio, TV, or in books, is now being presented or can be accessed by computer networks. or looking at this development in another way computer technology has almost caught up with the broadcasters. The drive to deliver multimedia information over a computer network is fuelled by protagonists of the Information Superhighway who need multimedia to justify the requirement for the highway. Multimedia producers are also looking for a wider market and lecturers are excited both by the new learning environments offered and possible efficiency gains.

7.1. NETWORKED MULTIMEDIA APPLICATIONS

Multimedia can roughly be defined as a technology that enables human to use computers capable of processing textual data, audio and video, still pictures, and animation. Applications range over entertainment, education, information provision, design e.g. CAD/ CAM, co-operative working such as video conferencing, application sharing, remote working and virtual reality experiences.

Multimedia Applications for computers have been developed for single computing platforms such as the PC, Apple Mac and games machines. The importance of communications or networking for multimedia lies in the new applications that will be generated by editing networking capabilities to multimedia computers, and hopefully gains in efficiency and cost of ownership and use when multimedia resources are part of distributed computing systems. Widening of access to multimedia sources and potential markets in multimedia, video and information are commercial driving force for networking multimedia.

The reality of networking multimedia is that : The characteristics of multimedia make heave demands on storage and transmission systems. Data compression can be used to reduce the demands of multimedia, particularly of video and audio on these systems, but usually at the expense of some loss in the detail compared with the source and at extra cost.

The availability of standards for multimedia networking, particularly for inter-working between Applications, the development of networked Applications, and inter-working between networks are essential to reduce the complexity and level of skill required in using multimedia.

7.1.2. An example

Using your desktop conferencing from Fujitsu which works on ISDN at 64 Kbps, and the Olivetti

PCC video conferencing, you want to do some work with a colleague at Imperial College in London who fortuitously has a Super JANET Asynchronous Transfer Mode (ATM) connection at 34 Mbps, and has a workstation with UNIX based desktop conferencing and a codec for H.320 compatible video conferencing. Hard luck, you can't. While the video conference systems are compatible, both use 11.320, the ISDN network cannot connect right through the ATM network. Also the desktop conferencing systems use different standards for sharing applications, whiteboards etc. and would not inter-work even if directly connected [1, 2].

7.2. USER REQUIREMENTS FOR MULTIMEDIA

7.2.1. Human - Computer Interface

The standards of reproduction for computers, which are desirable, have been set by the publishers of books, music, and Walt Disney cartoons and television producers. With the development of High Definition TV and beyond, it is likely that there will be a continual increase in the demands placed on computer based multimedia systems.

Multimedia Applications like any other application, appliance or tool benefit from being easy to use, with minimal training or self learning. The need for a well designed human - computer interface, which may be screen or audio based is well accepted.

7.2.2. Access, Delivery, Scheduling and Recording

Television channels can be changed at the touch of a button. On demand access times to computer information need to be below one second to be usable in real time. Alternatively the delivery of information at a later time is acceptable if it can be scheduled, as in a TV broadcast schedule, or a first class postal letter. Scheduling the delivery of multimedia information has not been widely implemented. Scheduling can have advantages for users over on demand delivery. In a learning situation times can be defined for class attendance by a lecturer. In open learning situations learners can control their programme by requesting a multimedia unit at a convenient time.

7.2.3. Interactivity

Interactivity, meaning the ability to participate in a video or audio process on a computer, by changing its behaviour or appending comments has become very important in multimedia. Some of this popularity stems from the perception of computer games as being enjoyable because they are interactive, and some from work done in education which shows that some types of learning becomes easier, and is retained more pregnantly if the learner participates in some way with the learning material. Computer based multimedia needs the same degree of interactivity that a school exercise book, or a laboratory experiment has in order to remain credible as a learning medium. The generation of computer based virtual reality is an extension of this process. The incorporation of interactivity is really the job of the application designer.

7.2.4. Educational Requirements

An Open Learner needs to be able to use any multimedia application at any time. However since open learning is often undertaken in centres, the use of audio and video require particular thought. Obviously several sets Sound Blaster driven speakers will disturb those learners working on a computer based self test. Similar considerations occur for users of multimedia in a class situation, such as a language teaching application. Not only will a number of students be performing similar activities at the same time on a network but the lecturer must decide whether to control the activities via the media of the computer. The use of multi-party desktop conferencing with the lecturer chairing the running of the conferencing session, showing selected parts of a video etc. is a case in point.

Distance learners or users of multimedia will also be capable of having same impact on a network as several students playing the computer game doom at lunchtime. Additionally the coordination of a learning activity must also be done by a lecturer over the network. So the role of the chair in multiparty video conferencing is crucial.

7.2.5. Cost

In education the main costs visible to multimedia users to date have been the cost of the computer platform, the CD-ROM, and software. Network costs are usually borne centrally within an institution, or by JANET nationally. The increased cost of providing sufficient network capacity and ability of new networks to charge on the basis of bandwidth used mean that individual users will increasing have to consider the cost of access when designing or using multimedia applications [3, 4].

7.3. ISSUES FOR USERS

7.3.1. Characteristics of Multimedia

Multimedia can be as simple as a few images with some accompanying text to a multimedia presentation using video clips, sound, images animation and text. Multimedia files to use a lot of data when in a digital format. Video is the most demanding. A PAL signal when digitized can require a data rate of 170 Mbps. Audio is less demanding but still requires 1.3 Mbytes for a 1 minute clip using a Sound Blaster pro system at 22 kHz sampling rate. Still images require use more data proportional to their size. Synchronization of sound and video is important. Sound is likely to break up if parts of it are lost or delayed in storage or transmission.

Video is less vulnerable to loss (depending on the application), still requires the entire picture to be on the screen at the same time and is also vulnerable to jitter. Jitter could be controlled in some applications if the sender of the isochronous video data time stamps each piece of data when it is generated, using a universal time source, and then sends the data to the receiver. The receiver reads a piece of data in as soon as it is received and stores it. The receiver processes each piece of data only at the time equal to the data's time stamp plus the maximum transit delay. Thus isochronicity of the video would be restored.

Table 20. Voice and video on an ATM network

Parameter	*Interactive Voice*	*Non-Interactive Video @ 30 Mbps*
Delay	200 msec	1000 msec
Jitter	1 msec	5 msec
Throughput	8.8 Kbytes/sec	4.1 Mbytes/sec
Average Throughput	3.9 kbytes/sec	4.1 Mbytes/sec
Packet sequencing required	Yes	Yes
Absence of packet duplication	Yes	Yes
Setup time	0.8 sec	15 sec

To accommodate these characteristics techniques used by the telecommunication networks to carry telephone and television traffic are required. These include compression of data, and methods of timing the transmission and replay of multimedia. Data networks and computers have been built in a different way (asynchronous) to telephone and TV networks (isochronous).

7.3.2. Compression

Compression algorithms and techniques are critical to the viability of multimedia networking. Uncompressed digital television required about 140 Mbps. Since few users have this sort of network access compression is the only hope for the widespread deployment of digital video and multimedia. Compression techniques depend on algorithms implemented in software or hardware. The use of hardware is important still to enable rapid compression, and also speeds decompression. Sound cards can implement proprietary compression, and software only video compression is available in products like Microsoft Video for Windows, or for UNIX workstations.

7.3.3. Storage

Multimedia requires high capacity storage systems. But over and above the continuous improvement in storage capacity of magnetic and optical devices multimedia raises issues relating to the format in which audio, video and data should be stored. A VHS tape stores video and audio in a structured analogue form. Digital storage techniques have hitherto used random access techniques, which do not suit the time structured format of audio and video. Since bandwidth is invariably limited in most networks users need to consider the option of local storage of multimedia data for subsequent playback. For instance the Internet is capable at present of delivering only low quality live video and audio. Local storage could enable higher quality playback for the end user. Storage systems are evolving to meet this requirement. For instance the ATML DiskBric is optimized for multimedia data streams and ATM interfaces with a 4 to 8 Gbytes capacity.

Storage devices such CD-ROM's need to be able to provide data at high speeds and in large chunks with low access times. Current CD-ROM's can transfer data at around 300 kbyte/sec or higher, hold 600 Mbyte of data and have an access time of around 300 milli-secs.

7.3.4. Bandwidth

Multimedia Applications, particularly those using video and images demand large bandwidths. However bandwidth for the foreseeable future will be limited. The limitations arise from the cost of installing optical fibre transmission, terminal equipment complexity and speed, tariffing regimes, switching speeds, and increasing numbers of users sharing equipment and networks. Photonic switching in trunk networks and the use of ATM on optical fibres will provide higher bandwidths, but the growth of networks such as the Internet demonstrate that demand will always exceed provision.

7.3.5. Quality of Service

The availability of multimedia resources places new demands on the service that a network must provide. The most important of these are the bit error rate, the packet or cell loss, delay and delay variation. Network resources need to be committed to multimedia data streams to accommodate the peak bit rate, mean bit rate and burstiness of the data stream. Until the advent of ATM networks users have had to live with the characteristics of the network to which they are connected. ATM provides the means to specify requirements in advance through an application. Users of ATM networks will be allocated different bandwidths and quality of service according to the application in use.

7.3.6. Platform Support

Multimedia also makes new demands on the workstations used to reproduce audio and video. Processor speeds operating systems, displays, storage medium and network interfaces and application must all be capable of handling multimedia. The Multimedia PC specification defines a 33 Mhz 386 SX processor with 4 Mbyte of RAM, a VGA graphics card, a sound card, a large hard disc and standard peripherals as being the minimum level of machine needed. Apple Macintosh and UNIX workstations already come with many of these features. Increasingly multimedia features are being incorporated into computer motherboards to reduce the need for plug-in cards. Considerable investment is needed particularly in education to provide large numbers of multimedia ready machines.

7.3.7. Inter-Operability

The inter-operability of platform hardware, networks and applications and multimedia formats is a major issue for multimedia users [4, 5, 6].

7.4. COMPRESSION STANDARDS

Uncompressed PAL video as a digital signal needs 140 to 270 Mbps, while uncompressed digital HDTV needs 1.2 Gbps. A digitised colour picture as 35 cm film resolution needs about 80 Mbyte. One minute of 8 bit sound samples at 22 kHz needs 1.3 Mbyte. These requirements are large for storage and transmission in computer networks. Fortunately many applications can live with video or sound that is not perfect. It is therefore possible to produce coding schemes that will drop certain information, or make a guess at likely values. Such coding can result in compression ratios of up to 200 times, so PAL video can be compressed to 1.5 Mbps. Compression must be done to a standard to enable decoding. However their are many compression methods. Microsoft Video for Windows, Quicktime are proprietary examples. A standard called JPEG is used for still colour images. For Video conferencing a standard called H.261 which is part of the H.320 standards family is used.

Further video standards are MPEG-1 and MPEG-2.

7.4.1. JPEG Compression

The JPEG (Joint Picture Experts Group) is the first international digital compression standard for multilevel continuous tone still, black and white or colour images. It typically compresses images to 1/10 or 1/50 of their original size. it is based on use of a discrete cosine transform and requires same level of processing to compress and decompress an image.

7.4.2. MPEG Compression

The MPEG (Motion Picture Experts Group) has so far defined two compression algorithms. : MPEG-1 and MPEG-2. A common misconception in that MPEG-2 is a replacement for MPEG-1. Each algorithm has been specifically targeted at different bit rates. MPEG-2 runs at higher bit rates than MPEG-1. There are no firm constraints in either algorithm and it is possible to run MPEG-1 video at very high rates. MPEG requires more processing power to compress video than decompress, so it is ideal for video film distribution. MPEG-1 chips on the market provide about a 200:1 compression to yield VHS quality video at 1.2 to 1.5 Mbps.

4.3. ITU-T H. 261 COMPRESSION

The ITU-T recommendation H.261 specifies a video codec for any number of 64 kbps channels between 1 and 30 combined. There are other H. series standards linked to video conferencing, and they are all subsumed under the general recommendation H.320. Video conferencing systems built to these recommendations should be able to inter-operate. The 11.221 and 11.222 standards describe the frame and signaling structure in 64 kbps channels. The channel can be shared dynamically between video, voice and data.

7.4.4. AVI, CDI and Quicktime

All these standards are proprietary. Digital Video Interactive (DVI) has been developed by Intel for the PC. A CD-ROM disc can store 20 minutes of motion video. It consists of two algorithms. The first plays back at 10 frames per second, the second at 30 frames per second. The faster algorithm requires specialist compression facilities. Hardware support is needed for playback of DVI.

Microsoft have a standard called Audio Visual Interleaved which supports small video windows at up to 15 frames per second. Apple also have a software based system called quicktime providing 160 X 120 pixel playback at 15 frames per second.

Phillips has developed a player for full motion video discs which can manage a data rate of 1.2 Mbps of video. MPEG based techniques are used [7, 8].

7.5. TRANSMISSION MEDIA

7.5.1. Copper Conductors

Copper conductors twisted together are the basis of the telephone network. As used in the analogue telephone network, with modems turning digital data into analogue tones, the data rate is limited to around 28 kbps. The introduction of the Integrated Services Digital Network (ISDN) led to the use of improved modulation and coding schemes. In standard ISDN the user can access up to 128 kbps of data at distances up to 100 metres from an ISDN socket.

Local Area Networks also use copper cable twisted pairs. Ethernet running at 10 Mbps can also operate at up to 100 metres or more, depending on the grade of the cable. These physical networks will be available and economic to operate for many years. For this reason considerable effort has gone into upgrading the network protocols that can be used on them for high bit rate real time multimedia. See below

A recent development is Asymmetric Digital Subscriber Lines (ADSL) technology which is aimed at using two wire copper loops at data rates of 1.544 Mbps in the network to user direction and about 600 kbps from the user to network. This is achieved by using better modulation and coding techniques. The driving force behind this technology is the delivery of on demand compressed VHS quality video to the home by Telecommunication operators wishing to compete with cable TV operators. If this technology becomes commercially available then the opportunity exists to deliver several ISDN B channels or even low speed ATM to the subscribers premises.

7.5.2. Coaxial Cable

Coaxial cable is still an effective medium to deliver multimedia. Cable TB networks use coaxial cable. BT uses coaxial cable to deliver some of its Kilostream services, and Local Area Ethernet networks can operate over coaxial cable to the 10 BASE2 specification. In general coaxial cable enables longer distance transmission at higher data rates than twisted pair cable, but is more expensive. One video conferencing provider has taken advantage of the potential additional bit rate available over coaxial cable and designed a proprietary video conferencing system for use over a LAN (C-Phone). Because for the higher cost of coaxial cable new LAN installations which are to be based on copper technology most often use twisted pairs.

7.5.3. Optical Fibre

Optical fibre transmission has been a strong enabling factor in the creation of a high capacity digital network on which networked multimedia applications will depend. On campus, the provision of optical fibre enable the creation of a high capacity backbones to Local Area Networks. However optical fibre provision to the staff desktop or student seat is still more on an exception than a rule due to the higher costs. In principal optical fibre can carry almost any type of traffic, at high data rates. It should be noted that there are different type of optical fibre, single mode, multi-mode, with different sizes, and attenuation characteristics. When upgrading from one technology to another, e.g. FDDI to ATM this may become important.

7.5.4. Radio Systems

Radio systems are likely to impact on multimedia in two ways. Firstly radio technology operating at microwave frequencies is available to provide wireless local area networks. Use of this technology for delivery of real time multimedia material should be treated carefully, because radio links are susceptible to fading, interference, random delays etc. For non real time use this technology is likely to perform as well as current Ethernet LANs. Secondly the introduction of digital mobile systems termed 'GSM' from a French acronym means that mobile users will have access to the same digital networks as fixed users. So in theory a mobile user will be able to connect to an ISDN users application, or an ATM users, with the only difference being one of speed. At present the bit rate of the mobile link is about 9.6 kbps. This may increase. With improvement in compression techniques the possibility of video conferencing on the move arises [9, 10].

7.6. SERVICE PROVIDERS

7.6.1. Public Telecommunication Operators (PTO)

British Telecom is still obviously the main provider of communications in the UK. Services such as Kilostream and Megastream from BT are already extensively use to connect networks. There are synchronous channels and can carry data, voice, and compressed video.

BT is also the only PTO able to provide ISDN on a national basis. New services such as Switched Multi-megabit Data Service (SMDS), Frame relay and ATM are becoming available, using the installed national optical fibre network as the common carrier. BT was chosen to provide the network for the SuperJANET pilot. Initially this was based on their 34 Mbps Plesiochronous Digital Hierarchy, but is moving to the 155 Mbps Synchronous Digital Hierarchy. BT are also providing Internet and video conferencing services. At present government policy prevents BT from offering video services to the home, but much of the technical work being undertaken by BT such as Asymmetric Digital Subscriber Lines (ADSL) technology anticipates the lifting of this regulation.

With the liberalization of telecommunications in the UK a number of other alternatives of BT are available. Mercury, Energies, Water companies and others are hoping to tap regional and national market niches. The basic technologies available from these operators is very similar to those of BT. One such market niche may be the linking of educational sites, schools etc. for the distribution of multimedia learning material.

7.6.2. Cable TV Providers

Cable TV networks are being installed in many areas of the UK, many of these have an optical fibre backbone, and hence have the potential of carry other traffic then television distribution. Whether this is possible depends on the equipment installed, and the architecture of the system. For instance a top down tree and branch network will be difficult to adapt to two way broadband services.

However a number of providers are offering analogue telephony service, with ISDN as a possibility in some cases. Potential exists for the glass fibre infrastructure to support Metropolitan Area Networks (MANs) linking educational institutions and related organisations [11, 12, 13].

7.7. LAN NETWORK TECHNOLOGIES

7.7.1. Ethernet at 10 Mbps

There is a vast installed base (about 40 million Ethernet nodes) of 10 Mbps Ethernet and 4 or 16 Mbps Token Ring Local Area Networks (LANs) using coaxial cable or twisted copper wire. Most new LANs used twisted copper wire cable. Ethernet uses a contention method to enable workstations attached to the same cable to share the data bandwidth on the cable. Nodes transmit to the network on demand, but continually monitor the network to see if another node is transmitting at the same time. If this occurs both nodes cease transmission, and try again later at random intervals. The throughput with such a system is limited to about half the available bandwidth or 5 to 6 Mbps. Multimedia file servers can be attached to such LANs. Both Novell and Microsoft have developed software to support video on these traditional LANs. Video in an Intel DVI or MPEG form requires 1 to 2 Mbps per user, so it is clear that only a handful of users can run video applications simultaneously. Audio requires lower bandwidth but is sensitive to unpredictable delays. For instance an intensive file transfer or video stream could prevent an audio application from transmitting onto the LAN for several tens of milliseconds, which is sufficient to reduce the intelligibility of voice. Improved performance is possible if LAN segments are divided up into segments with only a few attached users. Switched Ethernet takes this approach to the limit by enabling only one user to access a single segment which is then connected to a higher capacity network at a central hub by a switch.

7.7.2. Fast Ethernet

The IEEE has set out the aims of the 100 Mbps Ethernet LAN standard as follows :

* Line Rate of 100 Mbps
* 100 metre distance permissible to the Ethernet Hub
* Category 3 to 5 twisted pair operation
* Equivalent error rates to 10 Mbps

* Compliance with electromagnetic compatibility standards
* Simultaneous support of 10 Mbps and 100 Mbps
* Use of RJ-45 connector

7.7.3. FDDI

The Fibre Distributed Data Interface (FDDI) was the only standards based technology operating at 100 Mbps for some time. The first version of FDDI was developed as a campus trunk network for data.

Logically FDDI consists of a dual ring, but it may be implemented as a physical star. Key feature of FDDI include:

* Shared medium based on a token passing medium access control
* Compatibility with IEEE 802 LANs.
* Ability to use a wide range of physical medium including multi-mode fibre, single mode fibre, shield and unshielded twisted pair.
* Operation at 100 Mbps
* Support for 500 workstations
* Maximum fibre length of 200 km.
* Ability to allocate bandwidth dynamically so that both ‘synchronous and asynchronous services can be provided.

7.7.4. ISO-Ethernet

Architecturally, Iso-Ethernet, also known as IEEE 802.9 is a multiplexing of four separate channels of information: a 10 Mbps packet channel (P) with the IEE 802.3 CSMA/CD media access protocol, 6.144 Mbps of isochronous information organised in 96 B channels of 64 kbps each, one 64 kbps D-channel for signaling, and a 96 kbps M-channel for maintenance.

Additionally framing is added to allow for synchronization with a wide area network. The complete data stream is modulated with 4B/5B coding. The total bandwidth is similar to that used in 10 Base-T Ethernet so require similar cable technology and hardware to existing EThernet systems. A typical network will consist of Iso-Ethernet terminals connected to LAN hubs. The hubs may be connected by a backbone network.

Iso-Ethernet combines the best properties of current IEE 802 LAN and ISDN networks. Multimedia applications requiring isochronous channels can use any combination of ISDN B channels for audio and video according to the desired quality requested. Wide area interfaces from synchronous data channels such as Megastream or SMDS can be connected to the Iso-Ethernet Hub. Narrow band basic rate ISDN and Primary rate ISDN can provide Wide Area connections using Q. 931 signaling. ATM protocols can be added. The cost of Iso-Ethernet connections will be targeted to be competitive with existing high speed Ethernet cards.

7.7.5. Proprietary Lans

To enable video conferencing over existing LAN cabling some vendors have adopted proprietary solutions which replace the existing network hardware, but retain the cable infrastructure. On example is the C-Phone system which uses additional modulation above the 10 Mbps Ethernet spectrum to carry video and audio channels. Another technique is the emulation of ISDN over Ethernet CSMA/CD employed by TELES This is satisfactory for the video component of video conferencing but the audio component must be carried over the telephone.

7.7.6. Local ATM

ATM is really a network protocol because it operates at layer 2 of the OSI model. The physical transport of ATM has been standardized for fibre optics at 155 Mbps, 100 Mbps and synchronous digital networks. Standards are recently been approved for 51 Mbps and IBM with about 20 other vendors has re-submitted a proposal for 25 Mbps ATM transport.

The implementation of a local ATM network requires an ATM switch connected to a high-speed backbone. Initially users can remain on 10 Mbps Ethernet segments connected to the ATM switch. As requirements rise, direct higher speed native ATM connections can be provided. Use of existing Applications that run well over Ethernet should be possible in the connectionless ATM class of service. Effectively emulating an Ethernet LAN.

While some organizations will be able to provide optical fibre to the desktop for delivery of 155 Mbps, many have unshielded twisted pair (UTP) Ethernet LANs. The 25 Mbps specification may be worthwhile implementing in such situations if the cost of adapter cards and ATM switches is comparable with quality Ethernet cards. it is likely that the cost of implementing 51 Mbps over twisted pair cables with be considerable higher.

One such ATM adapter card for an ISA bus PC is able to operate over Category 3 UTP wiring. It providing NDIS-3, ODI and native ATM socket type application programming interfaces.

One pair of a cable is used for transmission, another for reception and token ring technology. ATM service classes are implemented in part by allowing different priority queues. Transmission is compatible with 16 Mbps Token ring physical components. A switch to support the adapters is available with 12 ports. Two port 155 Mbps nodules are available for trunk connections. An Ethernet transparency module permits LAN emulation.

Obviously this type of low cost ATM implementation is very new and will require evaluation, but other vendors are certain to follow, so the option of low cost local ATM is a real possibility. At least one video conferencing application developer has an interface in development for this type of LAN [14, 15].

7.8. WAN NETWORK SERVICES

8.8.1. Frame Relay

Frame relay is a connection-oriented service operating at n X 64 kbps or 2.0458 Mbps. It has evolved from X.25 packet switching and aims to reduce network delays, protocol overheads and equipment cost. Error correction is done on an end to end basis rather than a link to link basis as in X.25 switching. Frame relay can support multiple users over the same line and can establish a permanent virtual circuit or a switched virtual circuit.

7.8.2. SMDS

The Switched Multi-megabit Data Service (SMDS) is a new switched broadband data service. One of the first users of the service in the UK have been Super JANET sites. SMDS provides a switched connectionless data service at speeds of 34 Mbps (at present for connection of LANs. It uses variable length packets up to 9188 bytes in length, each of which carries an address in the E.164 format (ISDN uses this address format too) SMDS packets are transported in the public network using the Distributed Queue Dual Bus (DQDB) IEE 802.6 standard which uses packets fixed at 53 bytes. There is some overhead from this conversion process which reduces the bandwidth available to users to about 75% of the line speed. There are several access classes that limit the sustained data rate and burst data rate that can be injected into the network by a user. These access restrictions may result in discard of packets that exceed a certain limit. SMDS does not support timing. The higher speed of SMDS will be of benefit to multimedia applications seeking to transfer large volumes of data quickly, but the lack of a time structure will reduce the video conferencing quality obtainable.

7.8.3.The Integrated Services Digital Network (ISDN)

In the real world the delivery of multimedia requires a widespread network capable of delivering at high data rates. The current implementation of ISDN in the narrow band form is the best access and delivery medium available. ISDN is seen by many in the industry as the ramp through which multimedia networking will gain acceptance. The installed base of ISDN is growing rapidly. ISDN is able to provide connections throughout the world. In Europe the

Euro-ISDN agreements between operators is valuable.

ISDN offers point to point delivery, network access, and network interconnection for multimedia. Different data rates from 64 kbps up to 2 Mbps are commercially available which can meet many needs for transporting multimedia. Call set-up times are under one second.

ISDN will be the feeder network for broadband ISDN based on ATM standards. Initially the ISDN and ATM networks will be overlaid on top of each other, but users of ISDN will eventually be able to call an ATM user directly and be allocated an appropriate amount of bandwidth. The development of 'middleware' will enable applications to communicate over mixed Networks.

Although ISDN could be cheaper, particularly in the UK, it is likely to be cheaper than ATM connections and more widespread in availibility for a long time. It is therefore an important tool in bringing multimedia applications to a wide range of users. The idea that multimedia can only be delivered on broadband networks is erroneous as the assertion that only a Macintosh can deliver multimedia.

British Telecom are pursuing a strategy to make ISDN the preferred option for all multiple (2 or more) exchange line requests by the mid 1990s. ISDN is accessed through one of two services, named by the CCITT as Basic Rate Access (BRA) and Primary Rate Access (PRA).

Basic Rate Access (BRA) provides an ISDN user with simultaneous access to two 64 kbps data channels using the existing twisted pair copper telephone cable. The B.T. basic rate ISDN service is called ISDN 2. Each data channel is referred to as a B-channel and can carry voice or data. Another channel, the D-channel, operates at 16 kbps and is used for signaling between user devices and the ISDN. The total data rate of BRA is therefore 144 kbps. The two B-channels and the single signaling channel give rise to the term '2B + D'. BRA is also referred to as 1.420, after the CCITT recommendation. Basic rate ISDN is intended for low capacity usage, such as that required for small businesses.

Primary rate access can carry 30 independent voice or data channels, each at 64 kbps. The structure has a 64 kbps D-channel for signaling between devices and the network, and a 64 kbps channel for synchronization and monitoring. The total data rate of PRA is 2.048 Mbps.

Primary rate access is often referred to as '30B + D' because of the number of B-channels and D-channels, or L421 because of the CCITT recommendation from which it is taken. This form of access is primarily intended for use in situations which require a large transmission capacity, such as when organisations make voice and data calls through ann integrated Services PBX.

There are two standard ISDN connectors. For accessing basic rate ISDN, and RJ-45 type plug and socket is used using unshielded twisted pair cable. Access to primary rate ISDN is through a coaxial cable.

The ISDN passive bus, which can be a maximum of 1 km in length, is a cable which in user premises. It enables up to eight user devices to be attached to the basic rate ISDN interface. Since there are only two B-channels, only two of the eight devices can communicate at any one time. For this reason, each device must contend for access to the passive bus.

ISDN signaling information, carried in the D-channel, is used to establish, monitor and control ISDN connections between users as well as instigating the audible ringing or engaged tones.

The ISDN numbering system is similar to the contemporary telephone numbering system. Each B-channel has its own unique directory number which allows access to different terminal types. Each terminal type has an identity code, which ensures that it only communicates with similar terminals.

The equipment available for ISDN includes Terminal Adapters, ISDN internal computer Terminal Adapter cards, Video conferencing PC cards, and LAN access gateways or bridges, some of which ar based on PC cards or stand alone boxes. Products are available from in this country from the USA, UK, France, and Germany. The market for ISDN is most developed in Germany.

7.8.4. ATM

ATM uses small constant size packets to reduce and control delay. Control of the priorities of packets in ATM switches enables guaranteed delivery of information. ATM can emulate ISDN channels and Ethernet characteristics. ATM is seen as a universal technology which can be used over physical LANs and WANs and may be able to carry both asynchronous and isochronous data. ATM may also be delivered over ISO-Ethernet.

ATM network technology has strong industrial support and is already carrying traffic over the academic SuperJANET network. ATM can support different speeds, traffic types and quality of service matched to applications. ATM cells coming from a user are guaranteed delivery at the other end with a high probability and low delay. A cell is a short block of data 53 octets in length including 5 octets overhead. The performance aims are :

* A cell loss ratio of less than 1.7 X 10 - 9
* A cell transfer delay across the network of 150 micro second per switch. plus transmission and propagation time.
* A cell delay variation for one cell in 108 of no more than 250 msec.

ATM users have a dedicated connection to a high speed ATM switch. Switched virtual circuits are set up by the switch to a destination. Additionally ATM users can select a preferred network provider to service the connection.

ATM signaling establishes a "hard state" in the network for a call. "hard state" implies that the state of a connection in intermediate switching equipment can be set and once established it will be maintained until a message is received by one of the ends of the call requesting a change in state for the connection. As a result, an ATM end system receives guaranteed service from the ATM network. The ATM network is responsible for maintaining the connection state. ATM termination points must be responsible for changing the state of the connection, and specifically informing the ATM network to establish, alter, or close the connection.

Each ATM end point in a network has an ATM address associated with it to support dynamic connection establishment via signaling. These addresses are hierarchical in structure and globally unique. As a result, these addresses are routed. This allows ATM networks to eventually support a large number of ATM end points once a routing architecture and protocols to support it become available.

The variable and constant bit rate, connection-orientated with timing services are most appropriate to the transport of read time multimedia. However other services could be useful for transfer of multimedia material in less than 'real' time [16].

7.9. MULTIMEDIA AND INTERNET PROTOCOLS

7.9.1. Existing Internet Protocols

The Internet is a more of a phenomena than a network, but is important when discussing multimedia because a popular Internet Application, the World Wide Web is capable of accessing and displaying multimedia formats such as pictures, audio and video. The current Internet has thrived and grown due to the existence of TCP implementations for a wide variety of classes of host computers. These various TCP implementations achieve robust inter-operability by a "least common denominator" approach to features and options.

The system of connected networks which comprise the Internet has also been used to carry live audio and video. Extensions to the TCP/IP protocols currently used have been proposed as Real Time Protocols (RTP). Broadcast of audio and video has taken place on the Multicast Backbone (MBONE), by allocating higher priority to audio and video information from within routers.

The MBONE is being developed as a technology for low cost multimedia. Multicasting within MBONE enables multiple destinations to share the same information without replication. Internet routers an workstation software require some modifications to support multicasting. A virtual network has been implemented over the IP network to bypass routers which do not support multicasting, and to enable some bandwidth to be reserved for multicasting. however audio and video on the MBONE must still compete with other traffic on parts of the network. This limits the quality of both the voice and video obtainable.

Special purpose transport protocols have been developed. Examples include special purpose transport protocols such as UDP (user datagram protocol), RDP (reliable datagram protocol), NVP (network voice protocol), PVP (packet video protocol) and XTP (Xpress Transfer Protocol), XTP fixes header and trailer sizes to simplify processing and places error correction in the trailer so that the code can be calculated while information bits are being transmitted. Flow, error and rate control are also modified in XTP.

7.9.2. New Internet Protocols

A successor to the current version of TCP/IP Version 4 is being discussed. While some of motivation behind this is due to the need to increase the address space available, the opportunity is also being taken to review the need to increase the performance of Internet protocols, for multimedia Applications. The internet Engineering Task Force has resolved to move towards develop a replacement for the current

TCP/IP Version 4 called IPng (IP next generation_. Effective support for high quality video and audio streams is one of the critical capabilities that is being called for to capture the attention of network operators and information providers of interactive broadband services. Such additional features will also help overcome resistance to change. The intention is that IPng should last for the next 20 years.

The delivery of digital video and audio programs requires the capability to do broadcasting and selective multicasting efficiently. The interactive applications that the future cable networks will provide will be based on multimedia information streams that will have real time constraints. The largest fraction of the future broadband traffic will be due to real time voice and video streams. It will be necessary to provide performance bounds for bandwidth, jitter, latency and loss parameters, as well a synchronisation between media streams related by an application in a given session.

The potential for IPng to provide a universal inter-networking solution is a very attractive possibility, but there are many hurdles to be overcome. One of these is that a new deployment of IPng threatens the existing network investments that business has made and the other is that business users actually buy applications - not networking technologies. Some of the aims of IPng development relevant to multimedia are set out below :

Two aspects are worth mentioning. First, the quality of service parameters are not known ahead of time, and hence the network will have to include flexible capabilities for defining these parameters.

For instance, MPEG-2 packetised video might have to be described differently than G.721 PCM packetised voice, although both data streams are real time traffic channels.

Network media speeds are constantly increasing. It is essential that the Internet switching elements (routers) be able to keep up with the media speeds. A proper IPng router should be capable of routing IPng traffic over links at speeds that are capable of fully utilizing an ATM switch on the link.

Processing of the IPng header, and subsequent headers (such as the transport header), can be made more efficient by aligning fields on their natural boundaries and making header lengths integral multiples of typical word lengths in order to preserve alignment in following headers. Optimising the header's fields and lengths only for today's processors may not be sufficient for the long term. Processor word and cache-line lengths, and memory widths are constantly increasing.

There are now many different LAN, MAN and WAN media, with individual link speeds ranging from a ones-of-bits per second to hundreds of gigabits per second. There will be multiple-access and point-to-point links on a switched and permanent basis. At a minimum, media running at 500 gigabits per second will be commonly available within 10 years. Switched circuits include both "permanent" connections such as X.25 and Frame Relay services and "temporary" types of dial up connections similar to today's SLIP and dial up PPP services, and perhaps, ATM SVCs. Any IPng will need to operate over ATM. However, IPng still must be able to operate over other, more "traditional" network media. A host on an ATM network must be able to inter-operate with a host on another, non-ATM, medium.

7.9.3. Internet Protocols and ATM

ATM is a link level technology which provides the potential capability for applications at the TCP level to map to a single ATM virtual circuit for transport across an ATM network(s) customised to the network performance and traffic requirements for that application. The future Internet will be comprised of both conventional and "sophisticated" link technologies. The "sophisticated" features of link layers like ATM need to be incorporated into an internet where data travels not only across an ATM network but also several other existing LAN and WAN technologies.

An ATM virtual circuit is established based upon a user's traffic characteristics and network performance objectives. Theses characteristics which include delay and throughput requirements can only be defined by the application level as opposed to the inter - networking (IPng) level. For instance, a file transfer application transferring a 100 Mbyte file has very different link level performance requirements than a video application. The former requires a high throughput and low error rate connection whereas the latter requires a guaranteed bit rate. Applications will be responsible for reserving the required type of connection from the ATM link.

7.9.4. ITU-T Standards

The ITU-T is working on the 1.374 standard 'Network Capabilities to Support Multimedia Services'. This will cover service control, connection management, service management, and multimedia interaction for networks carrying multimedia traffic. Multimedia application programming interfaces (APIs) will need to be able to interface to this standard [17].

7.10. MULTIMEDIA PROGRAMMING INTERFACES

7.10.1. Design Issues

There are conflicting realities to consider when designing a common multimedia architecture :

* It is desirable to have a single architecture or protocol stack for multimedia and networks.
* In practice there will always be more than one protocol stack.
* Even within a single successful architecture forces of evolution will lead to periods of multiple protocols.

The fact that the Internet was based on a single, common, virtual network service (IP) allowed a ubiquitous underlying communication infrastructure to develop upon which a set of services could be provided to the user. The also allowed for a large market to develop for applications, which were built upon the underlying communications.

When there is a single common layer the selection of Applications becomes the province of the end-user rather than the intermediate network provider such as a telecommunications, cable operator or computer services department. By having this common underlying infrastructure, users are able to select their desired/required application services based on their unique needs, with assurance that the intermediate networking service will support their communication requirements.

7.10.2. Multimedia Communication Models

In fact the Multimedia Communications Forum (MMCF) are developing a reference model or multimedia architecture to allow easy application development for independent software producers. The first result of this work will be Transport Services Interface, which will be a type of multimedia. Winsocket specification, able to negotiate bandwidth, delay, priority and other quality of service parameters required by multimedia. AT & T, Intel, Motorola, National Semiconductor, and Seimens are some of the companies involved. The MMCF work is intended to complement the work of the Interactive Multimedia Association which has initiated a compatibility project to develop solutions to multimedia cross platform compatibility project to develop solutions to multimedia cross platform compatibility issues. The objectives of the MMCF Architecture Reference Model are to provide:

* End to end networked multimedia communication solutions independent of applications and transport technologies
* Extensible Application Programming Interfaces and Protocol Infrastructure to support to end multi-vendor inter-operability
* Support horizontal and vertical integration of Applications.
* Support distributed networking and computing architecture.
* Easy application development for independent software developers.

The MMCF have developed a concept of Middleware as part of the Multimedia Architecture

Reference Model. Middleware is a suite of applications, functions and programming interfaces the reside above the transport level in the OSI stack, but below the application level. The interface from the Middleware domain to the application and transport levels will be via application programming interfaces (APIs). It is not clear if the OSI presentation and session layers will be part of this architecture.

7.10.3. First Implementations

Implementation of TSI is expected by the end of 1995. The API primitives include :

* Administration - e.g. socket, bin, close, register
* Communications Session - e.g. listen, look, connect, multicast, join
* Information Transfer - e.g. receive, send
* Supplementary - e.g. hold, retrieve, conference, add, drop, transfer
* Quality of Service - e.g. priority, message size, bit rate, burst rate, delay, delay variation, cost, configuration, symmetry, reliability, type of service, security, negotiation.

IBM has designed Lakes Architecture for Collaborative Networking. This is meant to be an open platform for personal video conferencing. However the package includes the IBM Person to Person application. Lakes was not designed around audio or video Applications but claims to be capable of handling both. Lakes features are outlined below :

Multimedia Communications Logical channels between Applications, quality of service, synchronisation and data conversion, and call management.

Device Independence for audio, video, clipboard, display and capture.

Resource Manager Management of communications and collaborating applications.

Programming Interface For interface to file systems and network directory services. Lakes also claims to inter - operate with the H.320 and T.120 video conferencing/multi party conferencing standards. Lakes is probably the first of several attempts that twill be made to create tools to handle multimedia communications.

7.11. NETWORKED MULTIMEDIA APPLICATIONS DESIGN

7.11.1. Real Time Multimedia Applications

A number of real time Applications are available for use over networks based on computers, which are capable using audio or video. The two networks over which applications have been developed to date include ISDN, Local Area Networks, and Local Area Networks connected over high speed ATM or SMDS connections. The table below summarises the most important applications with examples.

7.11.1.1. Desk Top Conferencing

Desk Top Conferencing is a means of working with a remote user on their computer running the same application. Typically a drawing or spreadsheet will be transmitted via the ISDN line. A voice conversation between the two users can be held at the same time. Within desk top conferencing remote control of a computer is possible. Since these applications must reproduce the screen of a PC on another, the speed of the connection between the two

Table 21. Real Time Multimedia Applications

Applications	*ISDN*	*LAN's*
Desk Top Conferencing	Proprietary Desktop conferencing systems	wb.. an Internet white board tool, proprietary software.
Video Conferencing	H.320 video conferencing tool,	vat ... A visual audio internet ivs ... video conferencing software
Video Mail	Based on H.320 video conferencing	X.400 and MIME electronic mail with video content.
Remote Image viewing and manipulation	Medical Applications, eg X-Rays images	Medical Applications. Multicast of JPEG Satellite
Information Kiosks	Proprietary systems	
Distance Learning	File Server Access	File Server Access

computers is important. Products are available from Fujitsu for LAN and ISDN use and IBM (Person to Person). Desktop conferencing is also available over some of the video conferencing produces such as the Olivetti PCC.

The standardisation of multimedia Conferencing using the T.120 series of International Telecommunication Union standards is now widely accepted. Products based on these standards are likely to appear on the market next year from several manufactures. The applicability of the T.120 standards will not be limited to WAN or ISDN networks, but will be appropriate to Local Area Networks too.

7.11.1.2. Video Conferencing or Videophone Products

Until recently the only implementations of video over the telephone network have been poor quality video phones or very expensive video conferencing for executives.

Most of these products will provide ISDN applications such as file transfer, but the additional facility of a quarter screen video picture of the caller will be available in colour. Compression techniques are used to improve the quality of moving pictures. Sadly these some products use different compression methods so they cannot communicate with each other. But with manufactures moving to the H.320 series of compression standards, at least for video phone communications this situation may improve. Other standards e.g. MPEG are be better for straight video broadcast.

7.11.1.3. Video Mail

Video mail can be delivered via X.400 mail, or Internet mail with MIME extensions for file attachments. Obviously transmission times can be longer. An appropriate viewer (hardware or software) is then needed to replay the mail.

An alternative approach has been taken by Olivetti, who will release in 1995 extensions to the PCC video conferencing system. These extensions will enable video and voice messages to be left on a PC for viewing by a local or remote user connected over ISDN.

7.11.1.4. Image Viewing

An image database is considered to be a useful application for attachment to existing databases, or for standalone use. Products have been design for both general use and access via ISDN. Most products are designed not as stand alone image viewers but as part of an information system or kiosk for tourism or specialist applications. An example of the latter is a system from On Demand Information which markets a database for the building industry, accessible over ISDN.

7.11.1.5. Information Kiosks

Information kiosks are starting to appear with multimedia features. Information kiosks have commercial applications in tourism, government information and education. Extensive multimedia material can be held on local hard discs and updated at regular intervals, manually or via a network connection such as ISDN. The Olivetti PCC video conferencing system allows video conferencing to be incorporated in the design of an information kiosk. All the functions of the system can be programmed from within a high level language such as C++, Toolbook or Visual Basic.

7.11.1.6. Distance Learning

Distance learning Applications can held on a network file server. They can then be accessed from the local LAN or by ISDN. The high speed of ISDN means that the remote connection of PC's to LANs is now viable. The response of a distance learning application running over ISDN instead of a local LAN will depend on its design and the amount of visual material. Transfer of audio material will also take time and require a remote workstation set up for audio playback.

A remote access connection over ISDN to a LAN can be set up in three ways :

(a) Setting up a serial synchronous or asynchronous connection using terminal adapters to link the PC into a conventional LAM bridge or router.

(b) Placing an ISDN card in the remote PC and a similar card in a dedicated PC which is also connected to the LAN via an Ethernet card. The latter then acts as a dedicated gateway and is sometimes sold as a dedicated box.

(c) Placing an ISDN card in the PC and a similar card in a server for the LAN.

All of these methods require appropriate software to be run on the PC and gateway/server. LAN access is available for the NOvell IPX and TCP/IP protocols, for Ethernet and Token Ring LANs.

Distance learning can take many forms as

pioneered by the Open University in the UK. The development in he communications technology and computer systems has resulted in an increase interest towards the support of this mode of study using multimedia. One such project was conducted at the California State University at Chico. The trails aimed to assess the viability of using Integrated Services Digital Networks (ISDN) Basic Rate Interface (BRI) 128 Kbits/s) for transmission of voice, data, and video. The distance learning trial was divided into several phases. Phase I involved a point-to point trial between two locations. Phase II demonstrated the interlocated access transport connectivity. While phase III involved the use of networked-based bridging equipment to accommodate simultaneous instruction to three separate classes. The evaluation of the experiment has found the followings :

* Audio quality is very important. Even though the video, still image, and graphics media are available, the overall perception of the service is greatly affected by the quality of the voice communications.
* For distance learning Applications, the ISDN bandwidth of 112/128 kb/s delivers adequate real-time video quality.
* Animated graphics, audio, and two-way video are effective ways to instruct students in remote classes.

7.11.2. Non-Real Time Multimedia Applications

A number of non-real time multimedia applications are available for use over Networks which can support audio or video. The table below summarises the most important applications.

7.11.2.1. File Transfer

For LANs the de facto file transfer standard is the TCP/IP application FTP.

7.11.2.2. World Wide Web

Information provision is increasingly moving away from text to graphical interfaces with a multimedia content. The World Wide Web is an example. The World Wide Web has rapidly gained interest through its client implementations such as Mosaic. The delivery of multimedia requires a widespread network capable of delivering at high data rates. Paradoxically, on the Internet, the embryonic 'Super Highway' many thousands of users have to compete to use links which are rarely above 2 Mbps in capacity.

The interesting feature of ISDN for World Wide Web users is that an ISDN channel offers at least 64 kbps which is dedicated to one use. ISDN in the narrow band form is the most widely available access and delivery medium available. Using remote LAN access products running TCP/IP, it is also relatively easy to implement.

ISDN is seen by many in the industry as the ramp through which multimedia networking will gain acceptance. The installed base of ISDN is growing rapidly. ISDN is able to provide connections throughout the world. In Europe there are 'Euro-ISDN] agreements between operators . In the USA the use of the Web is driving the growth of ISDN in some states.

Although ISDN could be cheaper, particularly

Table 22. Non Real Time multimedia applications

Application	*ISDN*	*LAN's*
File Transfer	Various standards	Internet or OSI standards
Information Services with multimedia content	Proprietary or via World Wide Web (WWW)	Any networkable information system or WWW technologies
Multimedia Mail	Based on H.320 video conferencing	X-400 and MIME electronic mail with video content
Image Databases	Proprietary systems	File Server access
Information Kiosks	Proprietary systems	
Distance Learning	Remote access to file server	File Server Access

in the UK, it is likely to be cheaper than ATM connections and more widespread in availability for long time. ISDN will be the feeder network for broadband ISDN based on ATM standards. The idea that multimedia can only be delivered on broadband networks is erroneous as the assertion that only a Macintosh can deliver multimedia.

There are a number of issues in ISDN access to the World Wide Web. The relatively high cost of ISDN in the UK means that the user or organisation must carefully assess the cost effectiveness of their use of the Web over ISDN and participation with other organisations via LAN to LAN connections. The design of Web pages should make economic use of the ISDN call charging regime. This means that large images may need to be avoided, the size of a Web page in bytes can be dimensioned to fit within a call charging unit, and if your client can down load second level hyper-links response times would improve.

There are still major problems of software and hardware compatibility between different ISDN products. The cost of these products is till high but falling. ISDN access to World Wide Web servers on a LAN can be implemented in two way, routing and bridging.

A Bridge is used to connect two different LAN's that use the same LAN protocol such as Novel IPX or TCP/IP. The bridge acts ass an address filter, picking up packets from one LAN and passing on those packets intended for the other LAN. A bridge does not modify the packets or add anything to them. A bridge operates at the data link, Level 2 of the OSI model. A bridge uses the Media Access Control level addresses on LAN adapters to direct packets.

A Router is used to connect two networks that may not use the same LAN protocol. A router uses an inter-networking protocol which is understood by other routers and machines connected to each network. A router operates at the Network, Level 3 of the OSI model. A router uses and addressing scheme such as the Internet address scheme to direct packets.

ISDN connected LAN's can use either bridges or routers. Remote access to these LAN's is achieved by enabling the remote workstation to pretend that it is directly connected to the LAN.

Both routers and bridges need to provide basic functions to ensure reliability and security of data. The use of a bridge or router over ISDN also requires some additional mechanisms to reduce the cost of making unnecessary calls on the ISDN. At present this is implemented by 'spoofing' or fooling a LAN that wishes to send these packets to a remote LAN into thinking that these packets have actually been transmitted.

To connect LAN's which are closely coupled and within one organisation a bridge has some advantages and may give better performance. To connect LAN's operating between different organisations a router enables more effective management of addressing schemes and security.

The most efficient way to interconnect LAN's or remotely attach a workstation via a dial up connection such as ISDN is by use of the Point to Point Protocol.

At the end of 1994 about 27 suppliers had a bridge or routing product for ISDN. There are also a shareware PC based, and UNIX routers which may be able to be used over the ISDN. Some companies also provide a multiple serial line solution for access to a central host. The results of a survey by the Manchester ISDN Partnership indicate the following:

Performance The use of ISDN to connect LANs and enable remote access to LANs and LAN based services is feasible and offers bit rates to users of up to 128 kbps, which is adequate for many sorts of computer based 'multimedia' sessions.

Costs The running cost of LAN to LAN and remote access connections would be considerably reduced if BT implemented a per second charging scheme. The cost to remote users, of hardware and software is still too high for widespread use of the equipment by small companies. Cheaper ISDN products are available on the German market, but are only just beginning to appear in the UK.

Standardisation The implementation of the de-facto ISDN channel bonding standard is necessary for remote users requiring high performance. Standardisation of asynchronous use of Terminal Adapters above the speed of 19.2 kbps would enable a greater degree of high speed inter-working with ISDN routers equipped with 115 kbps Terminal adapters.

Inter-operability The availability of remote workstation synchronous access via PC cards to a an ISDN LAN router using PPP software would enable some degree of inter-working for remote users of different routers.

The implementation of remote access using TCP/IP protocols by router manufacturers is often tied to on software companies TCP/IP 'stack'. Router manufactures need to provide more options for users to use their existing TCP/IP software, which may be different from that used by the manufacturers. An inter-operability test facility for ISDN routers using PPP and remote access solutions would be beneficial to users. There are already limited claims of inter-operability by AVM with other products.

The most promising products are, in alphabetical order : ACOTECH ISDN for Workgroups, AVM Multiple Protocol Router, with Netways remote access. EU-System Maxpro Multiple Protocol Router, with Netways remote access. EU-Systems Maxpro Multiple Protocol Router, Jaguar Nile ISDN Router, KNX ISIS Bridge and remote access, Sonix Arpegio Ethernet ISDN Bridge, Spider Networks Pico and Mezza with remote access using Spider Integrator, Telebit Netblazer.

7.11.2.3. Multimedia Mail

Multimedia mail can be delivered viz X.400 mail, or Internet mail with MIME (Multipurpose Internet Mail Extensions) Extensions for file attachments, obviously transmission times depend on the network capacity. An appropriate viewer (hardware or software) is then needed to replay the mail. MIME is a way of transferring multiple objects in a single electronic mail. These objects can be text, images with a JPEG format, 8 bit PCM audio, MPEG video, application specific data, or postscript files.

7.11.3. Networking costs

Costs of implementing LAN technology and ISDN can very roughly be compared, excluding the costs of central LAN resources such as file servers

Network	Capital cost per user	Cost per MByte
LANs	£200	? very low
ISDN, Basic Rate	£ 800	£0.05 to £0.10

The cost of broadband circuit such as SMDS and ATM are an unknown quantity. Most of these systems are still at the trial stage. However the cost of sending information over a WAN is likely to remain high. The cost of provision of large bandwidth on LANs will also rise as users adopt multimedia. This will force users to choose the most economical access mode for multimedia.

7.11.4. Design of Networked Multimedia Applications

Multimedia can be transferred in three distinct ways, by a file transfer, as electronic mail, or in real time. Each is appropriate in different situations.

A file transfer can be initiated manually or automatically at any time. If done in advance of the anticipated time of use of the application, quite large files can be transferred. ISDN can typically transfer about 1 MByte of data per minute, which means that all but the largest multimedia applications, and large sections of video can be comfortably transferred in reasonable times.

Electronic mail systems are increasingly multimedia aware. Both X.400 and the Internet MIME standards can deliver audio, images, pictures and video. The recipient of the mail will of course need to have software integrated into the mail system which can recognise these data types and play them. Electronic mail can take longer to deliver than a file transfer, but has the advantage of being able to be used at any time in the absence of the participants.

A real time multimedia connection is the most demanding multimedia access mode. File transfer and electronic mail do not require a sophisticated, high capacity, or isochronous network to travel over. But real time multimedia demands the correct information at the right time. Users expecting real time pictures or sound are intolerant of delays in reception. Response times need to be of the order of one second. Delays in audio need to be under 150 milli-seconds to avoid echo.

Currently a lot of the media coverage of multimedia is oriented towards the possibilities of real time video applications such as video on demand, video conferencing etc., but it is likely to be applications such as multimedia electronic messaging and transfer of multimedia material between business that will become the workhorse of multimedia. In education non-real time use of multimedia material will also prove easier to set-up, and cost effective.

7.11.5. Design Guidelines

As with any computer application or teaching material creators of multimedia applications need to analyse the aims, objectives and environment in which the application will be used. Video or audio incorporated into a tutorial must have added value over and above over types of presentation, whether it be text, diagrams or photos. In other words the learning outcomes and type of understanding that is desired to create in the user of a multimedia application must be clearly identified. At an early stage in the design process the mechanism that will be used to evaluate the success of the application needs to be identified and a decision made about possible incorporation of testing or feedback mechanisms in the application.

7.12. FUTURE TRENDS

The evolution of communication networks from the current mix of analogue and digital access to full digital high capacity or broadband systems will occur. What is not clear is the exact path likely to be followed. Important networking issues will arise. With the availability at some sites of ATM technology, the use of FDDI for local networks at some institutions, and a large installed base of twisted pair Ethernet or Token Ring networks the migration path is not clear.

Access to ISDN, the availability of ISDN on PABX switches for internal use, the use of Metropolitan are networks to carry voice telephony and traffic and the use of LANs for telephony all throw up important issues of network integration.

7.12.1. Broadband Network Services

B-ISDN (Broadband ISDN) with its ATM technology, going through the process of standardization, is likely to be the most important candidate for the broadband multiservice network of the future. Much effort, worldwide, is being concentrated on building an understanding, through pilots projects, of this new technology [18, 19].

7.12.1.1. ATM Adaptation layer Services

Currently there are four types of adaptation protocols progressing through the standardisation bodies : ITU-T, ETSI, and ATM forum. These are AAL-1, AAL-2, AAL-3/4 and AAL-5. Each AAL type is aimed at supporting specific communication requirements such as connection-oriented, real-time issues, variable Bit Rate etc.

7.12.2. Future Teleservices

A number of other servicers (standards) are being considered by broadband standard organisations ITU-T, ETSI and ATM Forum.

7.12.2.1. ITU-T and ETSI Services

Tele-service	ITU-T Rec.	ETSI
Broadband Video Telephony Services	F.722	DE/NA-010029
Broadband Videotex Services	F.310	
Broadband Video Conference Services	F. 732	DE/NA-010030
Broadband TV Distribution Services	F.821	-
Broadband HDTV Distribution Services	F.822	-
Multimedia Distribution Services	F. MDS	-
Multimedia Delivery Services	F.MDV	-

7.12.2.2. Atm Forum Services:

ATM Forum Standardisation of teleservices are also at an early stage. The following services for Audio Visual Multimedia Services (AMS) have been identified.

* Audio visual Services and Multimedia on desktop: Conversational services with information types

such as moving pictures, sound, and data, This services is equivalent to ITU-T Rec. F.22 Broadband Video Telephony Service.

* Real-time Transport Service: The objective is the identification of a set of generic requirements for a transport service that support real-time delivery of digitally encoded video or audio streams.
* Video Conferencing: Conversational service with information types such as moving Pictures Sound and Data. This service should be equivalent to the ITU-T Rec. F.732 Broadband Video Conference Service.
* Audio & Data: Conversational service with information types of sound and data.
* Video on Demand: Retrieval service with information types that include moving pictures and sound.
* Broadcast Video Service: Distribution services without user presentation control. Service includes moving pictures and sound. This service should be equivalent to the ITU-T Rec and F.822 Broadband TV/HDTV distribution services.
* Best Effort Service is in line with the same work undertaken by ETSI/NA5 mentioned earlier.

BERKOM

The BERKOM Multimedia Collaboration service allows audio-visual conversions that consist of directory services, management and applications sharing. The BERKOM Multimedia teleservice supports multimedia message transfers in heterogeneous environment. In particular, it provides a framework for the presentation of multimedia messages and their compositions, sending and receptions.

7.12.4 Summary

7.12.4.1. Network Evolution In The Short Term

TV network have existed for sometime, data networks are only just beginning to approach their capabilities. Distribution of multimedia in the same way that TV is distributed is simply not possible system and a few high capacity links between centres. The Information superhighway is all about distribution of multimedia.

7.12.4.2. Future Networks:

The very different environments of wide area network and local area network have led the development of computer communications. Wide-area networking is high cost, low speed high error rate, and large delay. The design of the switch was dictated by the need to manage and allocate the bandwidth effectively. Both conventional circuit switching and packet switching are difficult to implement at higher data rates. In most current designs for local area networks where bandwidth is not expensive simplified addressing and switching has been employed at the expense of the effective use of the bandwidth. In particular, networks such as Ethernet use broadcast as the normal distribution method which essentially eliminates the need for a switching element (20,21,22)

Fibre optics has made high-speed information transmission possible. The problem is how distribute or switch this information when the intelligence needed to make switching decisions is operating in comparatively low speed electronic. For optical switching to be possible the switch must use very simple switching logic, require very little storage and operate on packets of a significant size.

REFERENCES

1. Evens, Phil, Business impact and implication of multimedia. In: Trulove, James. ed., *Multimedia networking handbook*, New Delhi: Viva 19 99. PP 1-1-5.
2. Adam, J.F., Houh, H., Ismert, and Tennenhouse, D., Media-Intensive Data Communications Magazine, vol. 32(8), pp. 60-67, August 1994.
3. P.S.G.Kumar and C.P.Vashishth. Ahmedabad, Information and Library Network centre(INFLIBNET), 1999.
4. Taylor, Alan and Madjid., A Review of Multimedia Networking, Liverpool: John Moores University, January, 1995.
5 http://www.man.ac.uk./MVC/SIMA/network/intro.html
6. Held, Gilbert., Placing images and multimedia on the corporate network. In: Trulove, James. ed., *Multimedia networking handbook*, New Delhi: Viva 1999. 13-1-13-12.
7. S.G.Kumar and C.P.Vashishth. Ahmedabad, Information and Library Network Centre(INFLIBNET), 1999.
8. Aptagiri, Devika V. Information super highway : the Internet. ILA Bulletin, 31(34), 1995, pp 70-81.
9. Blum, C., and Other., The Berkom Multimedia Mail Service, Working Document Release 2.2, Berkom, May 1993.
10. http://www.man.ac.uk/MVC/SIMA/network/seet2.html
11. Singh, D.V., Local area network: Its application in library management. Journal of Library and information Science, Vol. 20(1-2), New Delhi: Department of Library and Information Science, 1995. PP 84-91.
12. Conard. W. James., Broadband applications and technology requirements. In: Trulove, James. ed., *Multimedia networking handbook, New Delhi*: Viva 1999. PP 2-1-6.
13. Ibid., PP 1-12

14. Ferrari, D., Banerjea, A., and Zhang, H., Network Support for Multimedia: *A Discussion of the Tenet Approach, Technical Report* TR-92-072, International Computer Science Institute, Berkeley California, October 1992.
15. Wang, J.S.K. and Other., Dynamic band width allocation in broadband ISDN. In: Trulove, James. ed., *Multimedia networking handbook*, New Delhi: Viva 1999. PP 12-1-10.
16. Natarajan, N., and Slawsky, G., A Framework Architecture for Multimedia Information Networks, IEEE Communications Magazine, pp. 97-104, February 1992.
17. Bourne, J.Frank., internet Voice application. In: Trulove, James. ed., *Multimedia networking handbook*, New Delhi: Viva 1999. PP 12-1-10.
18. Singh, J and Kaur N., Digital multimedia: Impact on society technological developments and applications. In: Association Of Indian Universities. eds., *Information technology in higher eduction*, New Delhi: AIU, 2000. PP41-50.
19. Op cit.,(5)
20. Perey, C.and fieldman,., videoconferencing over IP networking. In: Trulove, James. *Multimedia networking handbook*, New Delhi: Viva 1999. PP 14-1-8.
21. Op cit(5)
22. Ibid.

8

EPILOGUE

During 1950s and 1960s, emphasis was laid on resource based learning, but in 1970s invention of innovative information and communication technologies pushed the libraries to accept non-print media resources in various range of formats. In the modern era of information based learning networking and multimedia computing and communication, libraries have entered into an entirely new era of the word Library had been expanded form merely 'A BOOK PLACE' to 'a media centre'.

Traditional library and information centres maintain the conventional media like books, video films, audio tapes, gramophone records, microfilms, and microfiche, which store the information material. It was not possible to the readers of the library to view different media at a time till recently. Now it is possible to the readers of the library to view different media at a time with the invention of multimedia technology, which store vast amount of data/information in electronic media and retrieve and present in more than one media to satisfy.

Regardless of whether the information is in printed media or electronic media, libraries store and maintain all kinds of information. Space is always the key problem to store he conventional form of information. Much storage space is required to provide to the users of the library with immediate access to he exploding data/information. This problem is solved through the multimedia products, which store vast amount of data/information in difference media using the author ware tools. Now the much talked CD-ROMs are going to be replaced with DVD-ROMs, which can store all kinds of media data/ information to the extend of 4-6 GB by using the compression technology.

Multimedia is a diverse and rapidly evolving discipline. Much of the activity central to multimedia does not takes place under the umbrella of multimedia, but goes by the name of more traditional vocations. Training graduates to be proficient in developing multimedia systems and assuring the long-term value of this training requires clear discernment reading the real nature of the multimedia phenomenon and understanding what sets multimedia apart from more classical endeavors.

Multimedia is not mainly about content authoring; many multimedia systems contain no authored content. Multimedia is about creating artificial environments that implement rich, interactive, multimodal information spaces, arising through a fusion of computer hardware, software, and multimodal data. An education in multimedia should empower students to be proficient in creating these environments irrespective of the target application, legacy data, host platform, or framework. To do this, students must be provided with in-depth knowledge of multimedia computing and communication systems in addition to expertise in software and multimodal data processing technologies.

The phenomenal growth of the Internet/WWW is the most exciting developing for multimedia Global communication facilities makes it possible to connect the libraries of various countries with one another. Further libraries around the world. Will be able to store the information resources in a way that was never possible before and satisfy the readers with information indifferent media. The concept of digital global library advocated some time back is the virtual reality now with the invent of INTERNET and today communication means Internet Multimedia.

In store, the library has been changed form print passed library to non-print media library, paperless library, electronic and digital library and multimedia library new with internet, and world wide web (WWW), it is heading towards becoming virtual or universal library. The role of the Librarian has also evolved from merely a custodian of books to media librarian, information. Scientist and net librarian who specialized providing services by exploring and information resources form the internet multimedia.

APPENDICES

APPENDIX : 1

INDEX TO MULTIMEDIA INFORMATION SOURCES

Audio:

All Music Guide
CWI Audio File Formarts Guide
MIDI Home Page
Audio(rec.audio)
Music Resources
Speech
True Speech FAQ
The Unix Sound System
Music and Sound Resources
Cakewalk Tutorial

Video:

Film and Vidia Resources Guide
MPEG Howto
DVD FAQ
DVD Special Interest Group
Frame grabbers for Linux

MPEG FAQ(HTML)

MPEG FAQ(vl.1)

multimedia CODEC Collection

MPEG pointers and resources

Images:

JPEG

GIF89 Tutorial

PNG(Portable Network Graphics)

Text:

Fonts

Text

2D/3D Graphics, Animation, VR:

Open GL]

BSP Tree FAQ

Computer Vision Homepage

3D Engines List

Animation(rec.animation)

PEX

Graphics, VRML FAQ

Virtual Reality Survey

The XAnim home Page

Computer Graphics on the Web

3D Graphics File Formats

2D Graphics File Formats

Authoring, Decelopment Encironments:

Macromedia Authorware Page

ScriptX

Macromedia Director Page

Multimedia Authoring Systems FAQ

PowerMedia FAQs, Tutorials

The GLASS MHEG Project

ToolBook FAQs & Maillist(listserv)

Education:

Guide to Multimedia Educational Material

Publishing:

Desktop Publishing Home Page

Music and CD-ROM Publishing Guide

CD Informarion Center

Photo CD Page

Broadcasting, Conferencing:

Desktop Video Conferencing Products

MBONE(Multicast Backbone) Home Page

PALplus FAQ

Satellite TV

Satellite TV

RealAudio FAQ

Distributed Video Production

Storage Technology:

DVD articles

DVD Sony

CD-I

CD Plus

CD Formats-Overview

CD-I(FAQ)

(German Kodac Photo CD Forum

Photo CD(Description)

Photo CD(kodak Archive)

Hypertext, Hypermedia,World Wide Web:

HTML, Editors

World Wide Web FAQ

A-Web

HTTP Guide

The SGML Open Home Page

Web Objects

Hypertext Basic Terms

Hypertext history and current research

Some Hypertext Products

Xanadu Home Page

HyperWave(formerly Hyper-G)

Interactive Web Tools

Web Tools collection

Gamelan Java Directory

Miscellaneous:

Acronym Server

Cable Regulation Digest

Document Understanding and OCR

Mobile Computing

MultiMediator - Multimedia Guide

MPC(Multimedia PC) Specification

Seybold Report on Digital Media

Amiga

Anime

Compression

Copyright Myths

Cryptographu FAQs USENET and RSA

Digital Signal Processing

Heidsite: Multimedia/Mac Info

Macintosh

Motif

Realtime Computing

SGI

X11

Software(freeware, shareware, generally sources, eventually also compiled):

Adpem(ADPCM codec)

AF(Audio File - an audio server)

AMOS Audio Tool 1.1(Sun SPARC)

BIT(Image Viewer/Editor, MPEG/FLI/FIC/DL player - SGI binaries)

Browser plug-ins

Continuous Media Toolkit(Tcl/Tk based)

CU-SeeMe(Mac video conferencing) CU-SeeMe reflector sites etc.

DIVE(distributed real-time 3D environment)

FreePhone multicast Internet audio tool

G711, G721, G723(audio codecs)

GIMP Home Page(Linux, SUN, BSD, HP, SGI)

GSM 6.10(speech codec)

H261 video conferencing)

hpcdtoppm(Photo CD decoder)

imtools(SDSC image conversion tools)

IVS(H261 video conferencing)

MAEstro(multimedia conferencing system

MPEG audio(MPEG audio Lauyer-1 and Layer-2 encoder/decoder)

MPEG audio(MPEG audio Layer-3 encoder/decoder)

MPEG Player

maplay(MPEGaudio Layer-1 and Layer-2 plauer)

mpeg_encode(Berkeley MPEG player)

mpeg_play(Berkekey MPEG player)

mpeg_player(extended Berkeley MPEG player)

MPEGTool(U. of Pennsylvania MPEG encoder)

MPEG-1 Analysis and Editing

MPEG-2 encoder/decoder

Multimedia WWW PC(authoring)

Network Audio(an audio server)

NEVOT(audio conferencing)

nv(video conferencing)

Picture Window(video conferencing)

pvrg(Stanford Portable Video Research Group JPEG, MPEG,p64 codecs)

qt2mpeg(Quick Tmie to MPEG converter)

scalable image/vedio encoder/decoder(Berkeley)

sd(Internet AV session director)

Shared Mosaic

Smacker Software Vision

APPENDEX:2

PERIPHERALS AND MULTIMEDIA COMPONENTS

Input Devives Mouse and Joystick:

Model	*Color*	*Compatible*	*Buttons*	*Internet Price*
Z-Bowxer GamePad	Transulucent	PC Compatible	8	*$7.50*
Internet Surfing Mouse	White	DOS, Windows© 3.1x,95, 98 and NT	3	*$7.95*
Z-Fighter Joystick	Translucent	Windows© 3.1, 98 and DOS	4	*$12.95*

Input Devices USB Cameras:

Model	*Compatible*	*Resolution*	*Video Capture*	*Internet Price*
Eagle Cam	Windows© 98	up to 320 x 240 and 352 x 288	up to 176 x 144 at 26fps	*$57.00*

Microphones:

Model	*Sensitivity*	*Frequency*	*Impendance*	*Internet Price*
Desktop	-42dB (0dB=1Pa, 1kHz)	2,000 Ohm	*$4.95*	
Clip On	-52dB$\pm$ 3dM	50-12,500 Khz	2k Ohm	*$4.95*
Headphone	101dB S.P.L. at 1kHz$\pm$2%(head-phones) 0dB = 1V/Pa at 1kHz -68dB(microphone)	20Hz to 20Hz(headphones) 20Hz to 16Hz(microphones)	32 Ohm (headphons) 1.5k Ohm (microphones)	*$5.95* *$5.95*

Modems:

Model	Type	Connection Mode	Vidiophone Ready	Supports	Internet Price
56k PCI PnP	Internet	K56Flex and V.90	H.324 and V.80 compliant	ASCII, Xmodem, Ymodem, Zmodem, and Kermit	*$32.95*
56K Fax Modem	PCMCIA	K56Flex	No	ASCII, Xmodem, Ymodem, Zmodem, and Kermit	*$85.75*
56K Fax/Data/ Voice	External	K56Flex and V.90	H.324 and V.80 compliant	ASCII, Xmodem, Ymodem, Zmodem, and Kermit	*$87.50*

PMPO Speakers:

Model	Built-In	Control Pannel	Internet Price
110 Watts	Amplifier	Power LED Indicator, Volume, and Stereo; Headphone Jack	*$12.00*
220 Watts	Amplifier	Treble, Volume, Base and Stereo Headphone Jack	*$40.50*

Sound Cards:

Model	***Capabilities***	***Internet Price***
Nightingale Module Kit	MP3/WAV, CD-ROM/LD/DVD, MD or DAT	*$16.50*
Nightingale Sound Card	General MIDI Sounds	*$38.00*

Video Capture Cards:

Model	Color Capture	NTSC	PAL	Protocol	Supports	*Internet Price*
Face To Face	256 - 16mi	640 x 480	768 x 576	H.245/H.233	125 channel cable TV Turner	*$69.00*
Genie	256 - 16mi	640 x 480	768 x 576	H.245/h.233	TV, Web TV, FM Radio closed caprtion	*$149.00*

APPENDIX:3

- ROM
  - Digital
    - CD-Audio
    - CD-ROM
    - CD-Interactve
    - OROW
    - DATAROM
  - Analog
    - Video Disc L-1
    - Video Disc L-2
    - Video Disc L-3
    - Video Disc L-4
- WRITE ONCE (WORM;DRAM,etc)
  - Digital
    - 14"Optical Disc
    - 12"Optical Disc
    - 51/4 Optical Disc
    - 3 ½ "optical Disc
    - 4.7"Optical Disc
  - Analog
    - Video(Check)
- ERASABLE (In development)
  - Digital
    - 5 ¼"Optical Disc
    - 4.7"Optical Disc
    - (CD-EPROM)
  - Analog

DRAW-Direct Read After Write

WORM- Write Once Read Many